Systemic View
Everything is Relationship

Eduarda Santos

Original Title:
Systemic View – Everything is Relationship

This book is a work of non-fiction that explores practices and concepts in the field of systemic psychology and human relationships. Through a comprehensive approach, the author provides deep reflections and tools for achieving emotional balance, awareness, and transformation.

1st Edition
Production Team
Author: Eduarda Santos
Editor: Virginia Santos
Cover Design: Studios VS / Mirae Koln
Consultant: Taren Solwyn
Researchers: Elira Denh, Cosma Virel
Layout: Nerien Glask

Publishing & Identification
Systemic View – Everything is Relationship
VS Publishing, 2025
Categories: Psychology / Systemic Therapy
DDC: 150.195 - CDU: 159.9.07

Table of Contents

Systematic Index

Chapter 7: Physics and Consciousness - Examines how human consciousness interacts with matter and energy, drawing on scientific discoveries that challenge a fragmented view of reality and point towards a systemic perception.

Chapter 8: Collective Reality - Analyzes human reality as an intersubjective phenomenon, woven in the interactions between individuals and social systems, where symbolic agreements and cultural matrices shape the perception of the world.

Chapter 9: Systemic Health - Addresses health as an integrated expression of relational, historical, and energetic factors, manifesting as a dynamic balance between the individual and the multiple systems they are part of.

Chapter 10: Systemic Diagnosis - Describes the practical application of Systemic Psychology in perceiving symptoms and conflicts, using sensitive listening to reveal the hidden dynamics of the family system.

Chapter 11: Family Constellation - Presents Family Constellation as a transformative approach that accesses, represents, and reorders the hidden dynamics of human systems, making systemic entanglements visible.

Chapter 12: Presence and Intention - Highlights Presence and Intention as structuring elements in systemic work, where the facilitator's quality of being defines the depth and integrity of the healing field.

Chapter 13: Quantum Communication - Explores communication as a creative act that models and transforms bonds, where each verbal or non-verbal expression moves energy flows in relational fields.

Chapter 14: Circles of Influence - Examines how relational reality is composed of multiple layers of belonging that influence thoughts, feelings, and actions, inviting observation of these contemporary systems.

Chapter 15: Transgenerationality - Reveals how we are part of an invisible network of bonds extending beyond individual biography, carrying silent inheritances of unprocessed events and pains from previous generations.

Chapter 16: Invisible Loyalties - Describes Invisible Loyalties as silent forces, rooted in family dynamics, that guide decisions and behaviors through the unconscious repetition of difficult fates from past generations.

Chapter 17: Illness as Message - Presents illness as a multifaceted phenomenon that can be an expressive channel of the body to communicate hidden truths, silenced pains, and systemic imbalances.

Chapter 18: Systemic Prosperity - Addresses prosperity as an expression of vital flow influenced by systemic dynamics, manifesting when there is harmony with the orders of love and recognition of ancestors.

Chapter 19: Romantic Relationships - Explores intimate relationships as a field of expression for dynamics inherited from family systems, where histories and conflicts of past generations unconsciously resonate.

Chapter 20: Inner Constellation - Introduces Inner Constellation as a way to access and reorganize systemic forces within ourselves, recognizing the inner field as a mirror of the larger family system.

Chapter 21: Daily Practice - Discusses the integration of the systemic approach into daily life as a continuous transformation of gaze, listening, and presence, recognizing deep dynamics in simple interactions.

Chapter 22: Forgiveness and Release - Addresses forgiveness and release as internal acts of reconciliation and liberation from emotional burdens and unconscious bonds with histories that do not belong to us.

Chapter 23: Systemic Self-Healing - Describes Systemic Self-Healing as a process of reconnecting with one's essence, activating internal resources to restore order, belonging, and balance in the psychic and energetic field.

Chapter 24: Quantum Reconnection - Presents Quantum Reconnection as a movement of consciousness expansion, where the human being recognizes themselves as an integral part of a vast living web that transcends individual experiences.

Chapter 25: Openness to Life - Portrays Openness to Life as the culmination of an internal process that dissolves resistances and restores the essential fluidity of existence, allowing one to live the now with presence and receptivity.

Chapter 26: Service and Purpose - Explores how reconciliation with roots and clarity of one's place in the family system naturally overflows into an impulse to serve, expressing authentic gifts in alignment with a greater purpose.

Chapter 27: Field Formation - Discusses the creation and sustenance of a systemic therapeutic field, emphasizing the facilitator's responsibility and continuous internal commitment to build an environment that favors the unveiling of hidden truths.

Chapter 28: Final Ceremony - Proposes the closing of the transformation process as an act of recognition and presence, using a symbolic ceremony to integrate learnings and mark the passage to a new quality of being.

Prologue

Some books present themselves as windows. Others as mirrors. This one, however, is a portal. A subtle—and yet visceral—call to those who already sense that something greater pulses behind life's events.

What you hold in your hands is not just a collection of reflections on human relationships, but a sensitive and profound map of the invisible field where destinies are woven, pains repeat, and healings are revealed. At this very moment, something in you has been touched. Not by chance, but by synchronicity. There is a silent wisdom that guides the right encounters at the exact right time.

You, reader, did not arrive at these pages out of mere intellectual interest. There is something more—a perhaps unconscious desire—to see with new eyes, to feel with new depth. This book answers that call. It offers neither easy answers nor ready-made formulas. Instead, it offers a gaze: a systemic gaze. A way of seeing the world that does not separate, fragment, or label—but integrates, listens, and transforms.

The reading that now begins is a crossing. A path where the boundaries between self and other become porous, where identity ceases to be rigid armor and becomes flow, belonging, interdependence. Prepare to be challenged. You will be invited to abandon comforting certainties and dive into a field where pain is a messenger, the symptom is a cry from the system, and love—ah, love—manifests with ordering and healing force, provided it finds its natural course.

Here, everything is relationship. Every gesture, every silence, every absence. Suffering is not a personal failure, but a reflection of invisible dynamics that cross generations. Repetitions are not weaknesses, but silent loyalties to those who came before. And healing is not just introspection—it is broadened listening, inclusion of what was excluded, reconnection with the soul of the system.

As you turn these pages, you will be enveloped by a language that is not content with the rational. It speaks to the body, to the field, to the memories you carry and perhaps do not even know. There is an intelligence here that communicates with something deeper in you—an archetypal wisdom that inhabits the collective unconscious and, when accessed, liberates.

The author does not teach from an ivory tower. She descends into the gut of the human, names what is hidden, gives voice to what was silenced, and embraces what seemed unnamable. Do not expect linearity. Systemic Psychology is a living organism, and this book breathes with it. Each chapter is a spiral of expansion. You will be guided through the subtlest layers of the systemic field, understand the intelligence behind the Orders of Love, recognize the echo of unlived traumas, feel the quantum entanglement that unites everything and everyone. And, if you allow yourself to dive in, you may feel in your body the strength of an ancestry that pulses not as a weight, but as a root. As a vital impulse.

The invitation is clear: do not just read. Allow yourself to be touched. Allow each concept, each insight, each metaphor to reverberate in your personal history. Realize how this book speaks not of "others," but of you. Of your relationships, your knots, your silences. Of that which you have not yet managed to name, but which perhaps you feel as constant restlessness, as sadness without origin, as fear that cannot be explained. This book arrives as a loving translation of these hidden movements that live in you—and through you.

Yes, this is a book about Systemic Psychology. But, more than that, it is a book about life, belonging, truth. A book that cuts through the superficiality of easy explanations and delves into the fertile ground of human relationships in their rawest and most beautiful form. Reading it, you do not just learn—you rediscover yourself.

And, in the end, something will move. Because the knowledge transmitted here is not content to be theory: it is a field. A field that touches, transforms, and reorganizes. A field that pulses with the strength of those who came before and with the hope of those who will come after. A field that, when read with presence and openness, reveals that the deepest wounds are also portals of reconnection with the sacredness of life.

Feel. Breathe. Advance. Because what is about to be unveiled can—if you allow it—change not only how you relate to others, but also how you inhabit yourself.

And when that happens, there is no turning back. There is only more truth. More wholeness. More life.

Chapter 1
Central Concept

Systemic Psychology establishes an innovative and transformative approach to human experience by proposing that the individual is not an isolated entity, but a dynamic expression of a system of interdependent relationships. The reality we experience is the result of a complex collective construction, shaped by affective, social, and symbolic bonds that connect us from birth. Instead of understanding the human being as a closed, autonomous unit, this perspective broadens the view to encompass the web of interactions that constitute our way of existing in the world. Every gesture, word, and emotion does not originate exclusively from within the individual, but emerges from the relational field in which they are embedded, as part of a living network in constant transformation. It is this expanded lens that allows us to unravel not only the internal mechanisms of the psyche, but also the invisible patterns that regulate our bonds and often unconsciously determine the course of our emotional, relational, and even physical lives.

By prioritizing the space between subjects – the place where meanings are constructed, affects circulate, and stories intertwine – Systemic Psychology invites us to overcome the dominant individualistic paradigm. This approach recognizes that family, social, and cultural contexts not only influence but co-author our experiences, beliefs, and behaviors. In this intersubjective field, the boundaries of the self become porous, allowing the constant transit of emotions, loyalties, and narratives that shape identities and sustain ways of being. Relationships, therefore, are not peripheral accessories to subjectivity, but central structures that support its formation and development. Understanding the nature of these relationships – their implicit rules, hidden dynamics, wounds, and potentials – is fundamental to accessing the deepest levels of human experience, where both limiting patterns and possibilities for transformation are revealed.

In this systemic horizon, reality ceases to be raw data to be perceived and becomes a co-created work, permeated with intentions, emotions, and mutual resonances. Experiences are not confined to objective facts but are amplified by the meaning attributed to them in the relational context. Psychological suffering, for example, can be read not only as an internal expression of the subject but as a sign of imbalance in the larger system to which they belong. Similarly, healing and growth processes are not restricted to individual changes but are realized in the redesigning of bonds, in reconnecting with excluded parts of family or community history, and in opening up to new forms of presence and listening. By adopting this perspective, the therapeutic gaze expands, becoming sensitive not only to what happens within the subject but also to the invisible and energetic atmosphere surrounding human systems. Thus, Systemic Psychology proposes a silent revolution in how we understand and act upon life: instead of seeking answers only within oneself, the human being is invited to listen to the network of relationships that constitutes them and to actively participate in the conscious construction of a more integrated, balanced, and meaningful reality.

Our connections – with family, friends, colleagues, society in general, and even the cultural narratives that permeate us – are not mere accessories in our existence; they are the very raw material with which our perception of the world, our behavior patterns, and even our health conditions are shaped. This book, structured as an in-depth course, aims precisely to unveil this profound dynamic. Throughout its pages, we will be guided to recognize how these bonds, laden with emotions, information, and energy, operate incessantly in shaping who we are and how we live. The premise guiding our investigation is bold and transformative: reality is not a solitary adventure, but a co-created symphony, a field of mutual influences where interdependent systems – families, groups, communities – constantly interact, exchanging meanings and affects that define collective and individual experience.

This systemic view directly challenges the Western tradition, strongly anchored in the notion of the individual as a primary and autonomous unit. While more conventional psychology often focuses on intrapsychic processes – thoughts, emotions, memories contained within the person – the systemic approach broadens the focus to include the space between people.

It is in this relational space that life pulses, where meanings are negotiated, and where behavioral patterns establish and perpetuate themselves. The family, in this context, is not just a group of cohabiting individuals, but a living system, with its own rules (often unspoken), defined roles, invisible loyalties, and a shared history that reverberates through generations. Similarly, our social and professional interactions form other systems, each with its particular dynamic, influencing our choices, beliefs, and even our physical and emotional disposition. Perceiving ourselves as an integral part of these multiple interdependent systems is liberating, as it pulls us out of illusory isolation and reveals us as active participants in a larger web of life. Health, from this perspective, transcends the absence of disease in the individual; it manifests in the balance and fluidity of relationships within the system. Conflicts, symptoms, and malaise can be understood not as individual failures, but as signs that something in the larger system calls for attention, rebalancing, or inclusion.

Deepening the idea of a co-created reality, we encounter the subtle yet powerful influence of the energetic and emotional dimensions that permeate all bonds. Human relationships are sustained not only by words or concrete actions; they are also woven by currents of affection, emotional resonances, and energetic exchanges that, although often invisible to the physical eye, are felt and registered on deep levels of our being. Who hasn't entered an environment and immediately perceived the "atmosphere" of the place, whether tense or harmonious? This intuitive perception reflects human sensitivity to these relational fields. Systemic Psychology recognizes that unresolved emotions, kept secrets, unprocessed traumas, or exclusions within a family or social system do not simply disappear. They remain as a kind of trapped "energy" in the field, seeking ways to manifest, often through physical symptoms, dysfunctional relationship patterns, or inexplicable difficulties in the lives of current members of the system. Understanding this energetic and emotional dynamic allows us to comprehend why certain families seem to repeat the same dramas generation after generation, or why we feel drawn to or repelled by certain people or groups without apparent reason. The reality we experience is thus profoundly affected by this invisible ecology of relationships, where emotions and energies circulate, transform, and seek balance.

In this context of interconnection and mutual influence, we can introduce, with caution and clarity, the notion of "quantum reality" as a useful metaphor to illuminate certain aspects of the systemic perspective. Quantum physics, by exploring the subatomic world, revealed phenomena baffling to classical physics, such as entanglement (where particles remain instantly connected, no matter the distance) and the role of the observer in determining a particle's state (the collapse of the wave function). Although we must avoid direct and simplistic transpositions from physics to psychology, these concepts offer powerful analogies for thinking about human relationships. The idea of entanglement resonates with the deep connection we feel with members of our systems, even when geographically or temporally distant. The notion that observation affects reality finds a parallel in how our consciousness, attention, and intention seem to actively influence the quality and dynamics of our relationships and, by extension, the reality we perceive. "Quantum reality," in this metaphorical sense, points to a field of vibrant possibilities, a latent potential that can manifest in different ways depending on the quality of our consciousness and the nature of the interactions we establish. It's not about a magical power to create anything from nothing, but the recognition that our internal stance – our presence, openness, the quality of our listening, and the intention we bring to our bonds – has a real and observable impact on the unfolding of events and the atmosphere of the systems we are part of.

Therefore, embarking on this exploration of Systemic Psychology is accepting an invitation to a broader and more integrated view of existence. It is recognizing that our identity does not end at the limits of our skin but extends through the ties that bind us to others and the world. It is understanding that the reality we inhabit is a living fabric, ceaselessly co-created by the dance of relationships, by the emotional and energetic exchanges that occur within them. Throughout this course, we will delve into the laws governing these systems, explore how the stories of our ancestors continue to influence us, and learn tools to navigate this complex relational web with greater awareness, responsibility, and capacity for transformation. The journey promises to unveil not only the hidden mechanisms operating in our lives but also the immense potential for healing and growth residing in the quality of our connections.

In a world saturated with stimuli and narratives inviting individualism, the systemic proposal emerges as a profound call for reintegration. It reminds us that every suffering, every pattern repetition, and even our most intimate longings originate not only from our inner world but also from what moves, or remains stagnant, in the relational fields in which we are immersed. This view demands listening. Not just any listening, but an expanded listening that extends to family silences, untold stories, inherited gestures that, even without words, shape how we love, suffer, resist, and move forward. Systemic awareness invites us to retell these stories with a less blaming and more compassionate eye, revealing that often, we repeat not by choice, but out of invisible fidelity to those who came before. This transgenerational fidelity, far from being a burden, can become a bridge to transformation. When we bring to light excluded bonds, repressed affects, and hidden loyalties, we create space for redesigning experience. We begin to live not just in reaction to what we received, but in creative dialogue with our belonging. This openness marks the beginning of a new posture: an internal disposition to take ownership of one's history not as a fixed destiny, but as a fertile field for conscious choices. Thus, the systemic subject emerges as one who recognizes their interdependence and, from it, builds their relational autonomy—not as separation, but as the capacity to connect more lucidly, integrally, and responsibly.

On this path, the therapist and the individual become co-explorers of an affective and symbolic cartography that transcends personal biography. The map is woven by encounters, by listening to collective emotions, and by perceiving the subtle energies circulating between bodies and stories. As we venture on this crossing, we discover that the reality we inhabit can be continually remade—not by denying the past, but by including it with awareness. And it is precisely in this integration that the most transformative power of Systemic Psychology resides: the possibility of living an existence where belonging, freedom, and meaning intertwine in a lighter, more human, more whole flow.

Chapter 2
Everything Is Relationship

Human reality manifests as an essentially relational field, where everything we are, think, and feel finds its meaning in the intertwining with the other. From the first moment of our existence, even in the maternal womb, we are traversed by influences, emotions, and meanings that do not belong exclusively to us, but emerge from the living network of bonds to which we are connected. The notion that the human being exists independently of their relationships is an illusion sustained by outdated paradigms that insist on prioritizing individuality over interdependence. The systemic understanding breaks with this fragmentary logic and proposes an integrative view, recognizing the relationship as the fundamental and structuring element of experience. Thus, it is not just about affirming that we relate to the world, but acknowledging that we are relationship in our essence—we are shaped, sustained, and continually recreated by the affective, symbolic, and energetic webs that surround us.

This awareness of the radical relationality of the human being leads us to a new way of understanding identity: not as a fixed substance, enclosed within itself, but as a constantly changing process, realized in the flow of interactions and shared experiences. What we call "I" is not a stable and indivisible core, but a dynamic construction, constituted in the presence of the other, in the stories we inherit, in daily exchanges, and in the silences we carry. Identity, from this perspective, emerges as a living collage of bonds, resonances, and loyalties, often unconscious, inscribed in our way of being in the world. Thus, understanding oneself is not just an exercise in introspection, but a movement of listening and deciphering the systems of belonging we are part of, revealing the depth of our interdependence and the mutual impact we exert in relationships.

To affirm that everything is relationship is also to assume that human phenomena—from the most intimate, like emotions and beliefs, to the broadest, like social behaviors and life choices—are inseparable from the contexts in which they arise. Psychic pain, interpersonal conflicts, physical symptoms, and existential impasses are not isolated phenomena, but manifestations of imbalances in the systems we participate in. Each individual carries within them echoes of the collective: unresolved family histories, unspoken expectations, traumas that cross generations, and invisible dynamics that update themselves in present bonds. Therapeutic listening, therefore, cannot be limited to the subject's discourse but must make space for the system's silences, for what speaks through the body, repetitive patterns, tragic destinies, or emotions that insist on returning. It is in this invisible territory that Systemic Psychology operates, illuminating the relational fabric that sustains life and enabling reconnection with the wholeness that only reveals itself in reciprocity.

The human being does not exist as an isolated, self-contained entity that subsequently decides to enter into relationships with others. On the contrary, we are constituted, defined, and, in a sense, created by the relationships we maintain from the moment of our conception. The very notion of a fixed identity, of a "self" separate from the world and others, begins to dissolve when we adopt this perspective. What emerges is the image of a being in constant flow, a node in a vast network of interconnections, whose essence can only be understood within the context of these multiple bonds. There is, therefore, no isolated identity to be discovered; what exists are relational constructions, identities that form and transform in the incessant dynamic of giving and receiving, of influencing and being influenced, which characterizes life in a system.

This understanding invites us to examine more closely the different threads that make up our relational web. Primary family bonds are undoubtedly the most formative. It is within the family that we learn the first lessons about love, belonging, loyalty, trust, and also about pain, conflict, and loss. Communication patterns, beliefs about the world, roles assigned to us (consciously or unconsciously), and the emotional atmosphere we breathe in this first environment profoundly shape our psychic structure and our way of relating later on. However, our relational constitution is not limited to the family of origin. As we grow, we enter other systems: groups of friends, school, the work environment, religious or spiritual communities, society at large. Each of these systems has its own rules, expectations, and dynamics, contributing to the formation of our multifaceted identity. We act and interpret the world differently depending on the relational context we are in, adapting (or resisting) the norms and roles expected in each system.

Perhaps the most intriguing aspect of this relational web is the existence of unconscious bonds with past events or with people we haven't even met. The systemic perspective, especially through work with family constellations, has revealed how significant events in family history – premature deaths, exclusions, injustices, secrets, difficult fates – can continue to exert a powerful influence on future generations, even if the story is not consciously known. It's as if these events create a field of resonance that affects descendants, leading them to repeat certain patterns, feel emotions that don't seem "theirs," or feel stuck in difficulties that defy logical explanation. This unconscious connection with the family system's past demonstrates forcefully that our identity and destiny are intertwined with a much broader network than our immediate personal experience. We are carriers of stories, legacies, and loyalties that operate in the depths of our being, shaping our choices and perception of the world in ways that only the systemic lens can begin to unravel.

A crucial point to understand is that relationships possess their own intelligence, a capacity to communicate and transmit information, emotions, and patterns that goes far beyond verbal language.

Relational systems – whether a family, a couple, or a work team – develop a kind of "collective mind" or shared information field. This field records the system's history, its rules, traumas, and resources. Communication within this field often occurs non-verbally, through body postures, gazes, silences, tones of voice, and, primarily, through emotional resonance. We feel the atmosphere of a relationship, perceive unspoken tensions, grasp implicit expectations. This relational intelligence is so powerful that it can profoundly affect our life choices, deepest beliefs, and even our physical and mental health, without us being clearly aware of its influence. A child might, for example, develop a physical symptom as an unconscious way of expressing unresolved tension between parents. A professional might feel inexplicably blocked in their career due to an unconscious loyalty to an ancestor who failed. A person might repeat destructive relationship patterns because they are entangled in an unresolved dynamic from their system of origin.. Recognizing this hidden intelligence of relationships is fundamental to begin deciphering the enigmas of our own lives.

Given this complexity, the importance of broadening our gaze beyond the isolated individual becomes evident. Trying to understand a personal problem, a symptom, or a recurring behavior pattern by focusing only on the person is like trying to understand a dance by looking only at one of the dancers. It is necessary to observe the interaction, the couple's dynamic, the implicit rules governing their movements.

Similarly, to truly understand ourselves, we need to direct our attention to the network of relationships that sustains, defines, and influences us. Who are the significant people in our lives? What are the recurring patterns in our relationships? What family stories do we carry? What invisible loyalties might be guiding our choices? What emotions seem to visit us frequently without apparent cause? These questions invite us to adopt the stance of a systemic investigator of our own existence.

Broadening the gaze means recognizing that we are not islands, but continents interconnected by oceans of visible and invisible bonds. It means accepting that our autonomy is always relative, as we are constantly being shaped and influenced by the systems to which we belong. This perception, far from diminishing our responsibility, increases it, as it makes us aware of the impact we have on others and the need to care for the health of our bonds. Therefore, the statement "everything is relationship" is not a mere play on words, but a profound invitation to transform our self-perception and our way of being in the world. It calls us to honor the complexity of our interdependent nature and to seek self-knowledge not only through individual introspection but also through attentive and courageous exploration of our relational landscape.

If we begin to understand ourselves as essentially relational beings, a shift in how we view both our challenges and our potentials becomes inevitable. Symptoms, repetitions, and blockages are not mere personal anomalies, but expressions of something larger pulsing through us. Each difficulty can be heard as a message from the system, a call for the inclusion of what was left out, for realignment with order and the flow of life. This listening requires sensitivity, a presence that welcomes without judgment and recognizes the wisdom contained even in the most dysfunctional behaviors. Transformation, in this sense, is not the correction of an individual error, but the loving reorganization of a relational field crying out for reconnection.

By understanding that we participate in multiple fields—familial, social, historical, cultural—we also realize that each relationship is an opportunity for healing or repetition. It is in the everyday interactions that we have the chance to break cycles, reframe loyalties, and create new narratives more aligned with our life purpose. Relational awareness invites us to humility: we are not in absolute control, but are co-authors of a living and complex dance, where each step reverberates in others and where each conscious choice can modify the rhythm of the entire system. This understanding returns power to us, but a power born from shared vulnerability, deep listening, and the willingness to let ourselves be affected.

Thus, recognizing that everything is relationship is more than a theoretical finding—it is an ethical and existential gesture. It is choosing a presence that takes responsibility for what it emits and what it welcomes. It is perceiving that our words, our silences, and even our thoughts contribute to weaving the field around us. And, above all, it is accepting that every bond, however challenging, carries within it the seed of a possible new beginning. By honoring this living web of connections, we begin to inhabit life with more truth, more listening, and more integrity.

Chapter 3
Systemic Field

The systemic field manifests as a real and subtle dimension of human existence, in which the bonds, memories, and dynamics that traverse the systems we are part of are inscribed. It is an invisible matrix, yet concrete in its effects, connecting all members of a human group through a network of information, affects, and loyalties operating on often unconscious levels. This relational structure transcends chronological time and physical space, encompassing past events, unintegrated experiences, and patterns perpetuated across generations. Within this field, each member occupies a symbolic position, and this position directly influences their way of thinking, feeling, acting, and relating. The systemic field, therefore, is not a metaphor, but an experiential reality that pulses in the interstices of human relationships, shaping conduct and organizing systems according to its own coherent logic, though often hidden from ordinary consciousness.

This field awareness invites us to understand that the emotional and relational reality of a system is not organized randomly, but according to subtle principles seeking the integrity and balance of the whole. When these principles are violated—whether by exclusions, injustices, disrespect for order, or abrupt interruptions of belonging—the field registers these ruptures as wounds crying out for reparation. And this quest for restoration does not cease, even if the original protagonists are no longer present: it updates itself in new generations, who then carry symptoms, repetitions, and fates that, at first glance, seem personal, but actually respond to a living collective memory. The field, with its own intelligence, acts as guardian of the system's history, ensuring that what was excluded or unrecognized finds expression, even if distortedly. Thus, apparently irrational patterns, disproportionate feelings, and inexplicable decisions can be understood as coherent manifestations of the latent tensions inhabiting the systemic field.

Perceiving oneself as an active part of a relational field carrying its own memory and dynamics implies a profound shift in perspective. This view expands the concept of individual responsibility, revealing that our choices, behaviors, and experiences are continuously influenced by forces transcending the personal sphere. It is not about abdicating autonomy, but broadening awareness of the invisible contexts conditioning our freedom. This recognition, far from being limiting, is liberating: it allows us to distinguish between what is genuinely ours and what is inherited, offering the opportunity to interrupt cycles of suffering and establish new, more conscious and balanced forms of relationship. By developing sensitivity to perceive the field's movements—its repetitions, exclusions, inversions, and hidden loyalties—we become capable of repositioning ourselves within it, honoring what came before without confusing ourselves with what no longer belongs to us. In this process, the field ceases to be an invisible script blindly guiding us and transforms into a living space of healing, reintegration, and personal and collective transformation.

Imagine an invisible structure, yet absolutely real and active, permeating and connecting all members of a given system – be it a family, an organization, a social group, or even a nation. This field is not a mere intellectual abstraction, but an experiential dimension holding information, energy, and a kind of collective consciousness of its own. It functions as a living repository of the system's history, guarding memories of significant events, emotions experienced (or unexpressed) by its members, rules governing interactions, and behavior patterns repeating over time. It is within this field that we move, feel, and act, often without the slightest awareness of its presence or subtle influences.

One of the most notable characteristics of the systemic field is its memory. It does not forget. Significant events, such as births, deaths, marriages, separations, successes, failures, traumas, migrations, acts of heroism or injustice, are recorded in this invisible matrix. These memories are not passive archives; they remain active, influencing the system's present dynamics. For example, the past exclusion of a family member, for whatever reason, can create a kind of "void" or "blind spot" in the field, which will seek to be filled or compensated for by future generations, often through the unconscious repetition of similar fates or the emergence of unexplained symptoms. Similarly, an unprocessed trauma experienced by an ancestor can continue to reverberate in the field, affecting the emotional or physical health of their descendants. The field possesses an internal coherence, a tendency to maintain certain patterns and balances, even if they are dysfunctional or cause suffering. It seeks the continuity and preservation of the system as a whole, and behavioral and emotional patterns tend to repeat until brought to conscious awareness, acknowledged, and eventually transformed.

To aid in understanding this idea of an invisible organizing field, we can draw a parallel from biology and life sciences. Biologist Rupert Sheldrake proposed the theory of morphogenetic fields, suggesting that living organisms are shaped not only by their genes but also by invisible fields containing information for their form and behavior. These fields, according to Sheldrake, possess a collective memory based on the repetition of forms and patterns over time, explaining, for instance, how a crystal assumes a particular structure or how animals of the same species share complex instinctive behaviors without direct learning. Although Sheldrake's theory is still debated in orthodox scientific circles, it offers a powerful analogy for thinking about the systemic field in human relationships. Just as the morphogenetic field would guide an organism's development, the systemic field seems to guide the dynamics and patterns of a human group. It would carry the relational "blueprint" of that specific system, influencing how members perceive themselves, interact, and repeat certain behaviors or fates. Introducing this perspective helps us conceive how information and patterns can be transmitted across generations non-genetically, through this resonance in the shared field.

The most direct and impactful consequence of the existence of these systemic fields is that, most of the time, we act within them completely unconsciously. We are immersed in these currents of influence without realizing it. We reproduce speech, gestures, emotional postures, beliefs, and even life choices that are not originally "ours," but belong to the history and dynamics of the systemic field to which we belong. It is as if we were actors in a play whose script was written by previous generations, playing roles and following plots we are unaware of. A daughter might feel compelled to excessively care for her mother, repeating a pattern of role reversal already present in the previous generation. A man might sabotage his romantic relationships, unconsciously loyal to a father unhappy in marriage. A person might feel deep sadness without apparent cause, which actually echoes unlived grief from an ancestor. These repetitions occur not due to character weakness or lack of will, but because we are energetically connected to these patterns present in the field. We act driven by invisible loyalties, by an unconscious need to belong, or by an attempt to compensate for past imbalances in the system. We feel the emotions circulating in the field as if they were ours, adopt prevailing beliefs as absolute truths, and follow well-trodden paths, all without questioning the origin of these impulses.

The fundamental goal in introducing the concept of the systemic field is not to generate feelings of powerlessness or determinism, but quite the opposite: to awaken consciousness. Becoming aware that we are immersed in these fields of influence is the first step toward differentiating what is genuinely ours from what belongs to the larger history of the system. It's like turning on a light in a dark room; suddenly, we begin to see the furniture, obstacles, passages. When we realize that many of our feelings, thoughts, and behaviors might be echoes from the field, we gain the possibility of observing them with new distance, without completely identifying with them. This conscious observation, without judgment, is the key to initiating a transformation process. When we recognize a repetitive pattern, perceive an invisible loyalty in action, or feel an emotion disproportionate to the present situation, we can ask ourselves: "To whom or what does this belong?". This simple question can begin to undo unconscious entanglements and restore a greater degree of inner freedom. Awareness that we are immersed in fields influencing us invites us to develop greater sensitivity to perceive their dynamics, honor the stories they carry, and actively seek our authentic place within them, no longer as mere repeaters of others' scripts, but as conscious participants in the system's evolution.

Understanding the systemic field is therefore essential for deepening our journey of self-knowledge and healing. It reveals that our psyche is not contained solely within our skin but extends into the relational space, connecting us in profound and often mysterious ways to our past and our fellow humans.

This expanded understanding of the systemic field demands a more refined listening from us—listening that goes beyond words and turns to the subtext of life, to patterns repeating without apparent reason, to affects returning with disproportionate force, to the heavy silences inhabiting bonds. When we learn to read this field, no longer as an immutable destiny but as a living landscape in motion, we become capable of acting with greater lucidity. We perceive that there is an intelligence operating behind each repetition and that, by embracing with presence what we previously ignored, we create space for something new to emerge. The field then ceases to be a prison of untold stories and becomes a place of reconnection with life in its entirety. In this process, symptoms cease to be mere obstacles and reveal themselves as messengers of what needs to be looked at and included. They speak of forgotten loyalties, broken bonds, exclusions crying out for recognition. Instead of fighting them, we can approach them with respect, asking what they wish to show us. Such an attitude not only transforms how we deal with our difficulties but also repositions us before existence itself: we cease being victims of a repeated plot and become co-creators of a new narrative. A narrative that honors the past without being imprisoned by it, that acknowledges inherited pains without perpetuating them, that roots itself in history to bloom in freedom. This is how the systemic field reveals its healing potential: not by exempting us from the influences traversing us, but by illuminating paths to integration. Consciousness, by touching these hidden layers, dissolves the veils of unconscious repetition and restores life's fluidity. Taking our place in the system, including what was excluded, acknowledging the forces sustaining us, and releasing what does not belong to us are simple and profound movements that restore order and balance. In this conscious repositioning, we stop carrying unnecessary burdens and rediscover a lighter, more lucid presence, more aligned with who we truly are.

Chapter 4
The Family Web

The family structure is the primary psychic and emotional territory that profoundly shapes who we are. From the earliest moments of life, each individual is inserted into a collective system predating their own existence: a field of bonds and influences woven by previous generations. This family system acts as the invisible foundation upon which our behavioral, affective, and relational patterns are built, functioning as a silent matrix guiding decisions, perceptions, and even fates. More than just a grouping of people united by blood ties, the family constitutes a living, pulsating, and complex organism where conscious and unconscious forces operate simultaneously. The experience of belonging, silent loyalties, inherited roles, and veiled secrets form the pillars of this invisible web that often decisively influences how we see ourselves and the world.

Each family constitutes a particular systemic field, marked by events, emotions, and dynamics transcending linear time. Even occurrences seemingly belonging to the past—such as losses, exclusions, violence, migrations, or bankruptcies—remain active in the family's emotional field, reverberating subtly or explicitly in descendants' lives. The transmission of these memories depends not on verbalized narrative but occurs through emotional codes, behavioral patterns, and repeated relational dynamics. In this scenario, ancestral influence is not symbolic: it is concrete, present, and often manifests in an individual's contemporary difficulties. Unprocessed pains, unrecognized guilts, and forbidden affects continue seeking expression, often using the body, mind, or relationships of new generations as stages for unconscious enactment. The result is the reproduction of emotional histories that seem to belong to the present but have deep roots in an unprocessed past.

Understanding the family as a system housing both love and pain, welcome and exclusion, inaugurates a powerful perspective for self-knowledge and healing. The family web, with its intertwined threads of belonging, loyalty, and destiny, carries not only the burdens of past generations but also the transformative force emerging from recognition. When the movement begins to look lucidly at this network—recognizing interrupted bonds, tragic fates, repetitions, and silences—the possibility opens up to reframe emotional inheritances and re-establish the vital flow sometimes blocked. Confronting family shadows aims not to reverse the past, but to free the present from its invisible shackles. By doing so, we truly honor the history that brought us here and assume responsibility for living our own destiny with more awareness, autonomy, and lightness.

If the systemic field is the ocean we navigate, the family is the main current defining our initial trajectory and often continuing to exert its force throughout life. It is here, in this cradle of relationships, that we find the origins of the most ingrained patterns, fundamental beliefs, and intense emotions inhabiting us. We can visualize the family system as an intricate web, a network of invisible threads woven over generations, connecting each member to all others and to the clan's collective history. This web is not made only of threads of light and love, although love is undeniably the primary binding force; it is also composed of threads of pain, knots of unrevealed secrets, holes left by unprocessed losses, and tensions resulting from past injustices or imbalances. Understanding the complexity of this web is essential for deciphering many enigmas of our own existence.

The unique dynamic of each family web is shaped by this inseparable blend of love and pain, inclusion and exclusion, loyalty and betrayal, shared joys and silenced sufferings. In every family, without exception, we find stories of strength, resilience, and bonds that nourish and sustain. However, we also find marks of difficult events: perhaps the premature death of a child, bankruptcy leading to total loss, forced migration severing ties with the homeland, an unrecognized abortion, a family member rejected for their lifestyle or choices, a secret about someone's true paternity, a crime committed or suffered. These events, especially when shrouded in silence, shame, or denial, do not simply disappear over time. They become part of the family field's implicit memory, vibrating like dissonant notes in the system's symphony. The emotions associated with these events – fear, guilt, anger, sadness, shame – remain encapsulated in the field, seeking expression or resolution in future generations. A family's emotional atmosphere is thus a reflection of this complex heritage, a mixture of present joys and unresolved pains from the past.

It is crucial to understand the mechanisms by which this family web exerts its influence on current members, often entirely unconsciously. One of the most powerful concepts revealed by the systemic approach is that of invisible loyalties. This refers to a deep, unconscious fidelity a system member (usually a descendant) maintains towards an ancestor's fate, suffering, or beliefs. This love, although stemming from good intentions at the soul level – the need to belong, honor, compensate – often manifests tragically. Out of invisible loyalty to a father who failed financially, a son might unconsciously sabotage his own professional success. Out of loyalty to a mother who suffered in an abusive relationship, a daughter might feel prevented from experiencing a happy and fulfilling love, as if betraying her mother by being happy where she wasn't. Out of loyalty to an excluded family member, someone might adopt self-destructive behaviors or develop symptoms mirroring the fate of the forgotten one. These loyalties operate in the shadows of consciousness; the person does not rationally decide to repeat a difficult fate but feels compelled by an internal force they don't understand, moved by a love that, being blind to consequences, ends up perpetuating suffering instead of healing it.

Another fundamental mechanism is the transmission of inherited traumas. Today, epigenetics begins to offer possible scientific explanations for how traumatic experiences can leave biological marks passed down to subsequent generations, but the systemic perspective has observed this phenomenon for decades at the level of relational dynamics and the family field. Significant traumas – such as those experienced in wars, genocides, natural disasters, situations of severe abuse, or devastating losses – create shockwaves propagating through the family web. Descendants, even if they did not directly experience the traumatic event and perhaps don't even know the story in detail, can carry the emotional and energetic remnants of this trauma. This might manifest as free-floating anxiety without apparent cause, specific phobias, a sense of impending danger, chronic depression, autoimmune diseases, or a persistent difficulty in trusting life or others. The descendant's body and psyche become, unknowingly, the stage where the ancestor's unresolved drama continues to be enacted. The pain that couldn't be felt, the grief that couldn't be lived, the anger that couldn't be expressed in the past seek a way to surface in the present, through the symptoms and difficulties of those who came later.

Associated with this, we have patterns of repetition. Observing a family's history over several generations often reveals the recurrence of certain themes, conflicts, or fates. One family might have a history of men dying young or abandoning their wives.

Another might show a pattern of women suffering from depression or having difficulty conceiving. There might be repetitions of addictions, financial problems, accidents, certain types of illnesses, or specific relationship dynamics (like love triangles or dependency relationships). These repetitions are not mere coincidences. They indicate the presence of an unresolved systemic pattern or entanglement still active in the family field, seeking to be seen and integrated. Repetition functions as the system's blind attempt to bring to light something left pending, to include someone excluded, or to restore a lost balance. As long as the pattern is not made conscious and addressed at its systemic root, it tends to persist, passing from generation to generation like an unwanted legacy. Once again, it's crucial to emphasize that these influences – loyalties, traumas, patterns – operate predominantly outside the individual's conscious awareness. The person finds themselves living certain difficulties or repeating certain behaviors without understanding why, often feeling guilty or inadequate, when in fact they are responding to much larger forces operating at the family system level.

Given this picture, it becomes undeniably clear that any serious journey of self-knowledge must necessarily include a courageous and honest exploration of one's own family history. Trying to understand oneself while ignoring the roots from which we came is like trying to understand a tree by looking only at its branches and leaves, without considering the trunk and, especially, the hidden roots beneath the earth. Our identity, values, fears, dreams, greatest wounds, and greatest gifts are deeply intertwined with the history of those who preceded us. Looking at this history, including its difficult passages, secrets, and pains, does not aim to find culprits or masochistically relive the past. The goal is recognition. Recognizing what was, how it was, and the impact it had and continues to have on our lives. Recognizing everyone's place, everyone's fate, the burdens each carried. This recognition, done with respect and without judgment, is profoundly liberating. It allows us to begin differentiating what is ours from what we carry for others, to symbolically return burdens that do not belong to us, and to honor our ancestors in a way that strengthens us, instead of binding us to their fates. The hidden layers of family history contain not only pain but also immense resources of strength, resilience, and love that can be accessed when we are willing to look.

Thus, the family web, with all its complexity of light and shadow, reveals itself not as a prison from which we must escape, but as a portal. A portal to a deeper understanding of ourselves, to healing old wounds limiting our present, and to achieving greater emotional freedom. By unraveling the threads of invisible loyalties, releasing echoes of inherited traumas, and interrupting imprisoning patterns of repetition, we create space for the life force flowing through our lineage to nourish us healthily. Honoring the family web means looking at it clearly, accepting its history as it was, and taking our own place within it with responsibility and love. It is in this process of recognition, integration, and differentiation that we find the path to transform legacies of pain into sources of wisdom and strength, finally allowing us to live our own lives to the fullest.

Chapter 5
Orders of Love

Family dynamics, though often shrouded in complexity and suffering, do not operate randomly. Underlying all human relationships exists a systemic intelligence constantly seeking harmony and the continuation of life. This intelligence manifests through universal principles governing bonds, and when these principles are respected, love—that essential force linking and sustaining systems—finds a fertile path to express itself healthily. It is these natural laws, deeply rooted in the structure of relational fields, that allow for the fluidity of belonging, order, and the balance between giving and receiving. By identifying these organizing forces, it becomes possible to recognize that much of the suffering experienced in families results not from malice or chance, but from the unconscious violation of these laws maintaining the system's cohesion and vitality.

These principles, named "Orders of Love" by Bert Hellinger, are not moral prescriptions or social norms. They are phenomenological observations about what keeps life flowing within human systems. When one of these orders is violated, even without intention or awareness, the system responds with warning signs: recurring conflicts, exclusions generating veiled pain, relationships marked by inexplicable ruptures, or even physical and emotional symptoms defying logical explanations. However, such manifestations should not be seen as punishments, but rather as expressions of a field seeking to restore its integrity and balance. By closely observing these manifestations, the possibility opens up to understand what needs to be seen, honored, or reintegrated, transforming suffering into a portal for reconnection with the essential order of life.

Perceiving these orders invites us to step out of the logic of judgment and into the field of respectful observation. When we understand, for example, that every family member has an inalienable right to belong, or that bonds strengthen when there is a fair flow of exchange, we begin to see more clearly the roots of certain perpetuating patterns. This shift in perspective not only broadens our understanding of family dynamics but also empowers us to make healing movements. Recognizing the natural hierarchy, including the excluded, and balancing relationships does not demand perfection, but awareness. With this awareness, it is possible to honor the past without being imprisoned by it, integrate what was excluded without guilt, and allow love to manifest freely and responsibly—thus becoming a force that heals, guides, and transforms.

Hellinger termed these principles "Orders of Love." It is fundamental to understand that these are not moral commandments or externally imposed rules, but rather phenomenological findings, observations about the conditions allowing love to flourish and life force to circulate healthily within a system, be it familial, social, or organizational. When these orders are respected, even unconsciously, there is a tendency towards harmony, growth, and well-being. However, when violated, tensions, conflicts, symptoms, and dynamics of suffering arise, affecting everyone involved. Understanding these orders is therefore essential for diagnosing the roots of many relational problems and finding paths to healing and reconciliation.

The first and most fundamental of these orders is the right to belong. Every person entering a family system, whether by birth, marriage, or through a significantly linked fate (like a victim or perpetrator of a serious act involving a family member, or even an important previous partner), acquires an inalienable right to belong to that system. No one can be excluded with impunity. The group conscience, or the "family soul," as Hellinger sometimes called it, does not tolerate exclusions. When a member is denied, forgotten, morally judged, and "erased" from family history – perhaps for having a fate considered shameful (mental illness, imprisonment, addiction), for representing unbearable pain (a stillborn baby, an aborted child), or for being overlooked (a significant first love) – the system becomes unbalanced. The field's need for integrity causes it to seek compensation. Frequently, a member of a later generation, without any conscious knowledge of the history, feels compelled to represent the excluded one. This can happen in various ways: the person might develop symptoms similar to the excluded one, repeat their tragic fate, feel an inexplicable affinity for them, or carry a sense of guilt or inadequacy that actually belongs to the system as a whole due to the committed exclusion. Exclusion, therefore, does not eliminate the problem; on the contrary, it perpetuates it covertly, creating entanglements that can only be undone when the excluded is acknowledged, honored, and reintegrated into their rightful place in the family's heart and history. Belonging is the foundation upon which the entire system rests.

The second order refers to hierarchy, determined by the time of arrival into the system. Those who came before take precedence over those who came later. This establishes a natural order that needs respect for clarity of roles and functions. Parents come before children; the relationship with the first partner has temporal precedence over the second; older siblings come before younger ones. This precedence confers neither moral superiority nor greater value, but defines a specific place and responsibility. Parents, having come first and given life, occupy a position of "big" relative to children, who are the "small". The primary function of parents is to give (life, care, protection, limits), and that of children is to receive and eventually carry that life forward. When this order is violated, the systemic dynamic becomes unbalanced. A common example is "parentification," where a child, for various reasons (parents' illness or immaturity, need to mediate conflicts), assumes parental responsibilities, unconsciously placing themselves in a position equal or even superior to the parents. Although it might seem an act of love or necessity, this inversion overburdens the child, prevents them from living their childhood, and generates resentment and difficulties in their future relationships. Similarly, when a new partner tries to occupy the place of the previous one, disrespecting their past bond with the spouse and the children from that relationship, disorder is created. Respecting the order of arrival means acknowledging everyone's place, honoring who came before, and assuming the responsibilities and prerogatives corresponding to one's own position in the system.

The third order concerns the balance between giving and receiving. For relationships to remain alive and healthy over time, a balanced exchange between partners is necessary. This order applies most directly to relationships between equals, such as couples, friends, or work colleagues. In these bonds, giving and receiving need to alternate and compensate each other. When one gives something good to the other, the receiver feels a kind of positive "debt," an impulse to reciprocate, perhaps with something slightly greater, generating a virtuous cycle of exchanges that strengthens the bond and deepens intimacy and trust. The same applies to the negative: when one harms the other, the need for reparation arises to restore balance. If, however, the imbalance becomes chronic – one always gives and the other always receives, or one always harms and the other always forgives without reparation – the bond weakens. The one who only receives may feel excessively indebted and diminished, while the one who only gives may feel exhausted and unacknowledged. In both cases, the relationship loses vitality and tends to break. It is important to note that the dynamic between parents and children operates differently. Parents give life, a gift so immense that children can never reciprocate in the same measure. The appropriate "reciprocation" from children is not trying to give back to the parents (which would violate the hierarchy), but rather receiving life with gratitude, doing something good with it, and eventually passing it on, either by having their own children or by contributing to the world through their work and talents. Balance here manifests in the flow of life across generations.

Contemplating these three orders – belonging, hierarchy, and balance in exchange – we perceive the profound wisdom they contain. They reveal that love, that powerful force moving and connecting us, is not sufficient on its own to guarantee harmony and well-being. Love needs a structure, a bed through which it can flow in an orderly and constructive way. Often, in the name of "blind love," we violate these orders without realizing it. Out of blind loyalty, we exclude someone considered "unworthy" (violating belonging). Out of a desire to help or a need for control, we place ourselves above our parents or disrespect those who came before (violating hierarchy). Out of fear of conflict or a distorted perception of generosity, we give excessively without allowing ourselves to receive, or receive without reciprocating (violating balance). These actions, even if well-intentioned, generate entanglements and suffering because they go against the natural laws governing relational systems. The love that heals, strengthens, and liberates is the one that acknowledges and respects these fundamental orders.

The good news is that systemic disorders, although potentially causing deep pain and manifesting in complex problems like chronic conflicts, serious illnesses, or repetitive failures, are not immutable sentences. The systemic field possesses an intrinsic capacity for self-organization and constantly seeks balance. The key to reorganization and healing lies in consciousness. By becoming aware of the Orders of Love and learning to observe our own family and relational systems through this lens, we can begin to identify where the orders have been violated. This recognition, made without judgment but with deep respect for the history and fate of everyone involved, is the first step. The next step is the movement of inclusion: giving a place in the heart and family history to all who were excluded, acknowledging the precedence of those who came before, seeking a healthier balance in exchanges. These internal movements, often accompanied by symbolic gestures or phrases of recognition, have the power to restore order in the field, release entanglements, and allow love and life force to flow freely again. The suffering generated by disorder can then be transformed into wisdom and strength, paving the way for reconciliation and a fuller, more connected life.

Chapter 6
The Systemic Unconscious

The systemic unconscious reveals itself as a deep instance of collective consciousness that transcends the linear logic of personal history and challenges the traditional perception of the self as an autonomous being separate from its family context. This invisible yet active field is imbued with emotional experiences, unresolved bonds, and significant events traversing generations, impressing upon descendants the reflections of old pains, interrupted bonds, and excluded fates. It is not a poetic metaphor or symbolic notion, but an observable reality in behavioral repetitions, dysfunctional affective bonds, inexplicable physical and emotional symptoms, and life choices seemingly guided by forces beyond conscious control. The systemic unconscious acts as a living memory field, where family history continues to manifest, even if facts have been forgotten, hidden, or never verbalized.

This unconscious operates according to its own laws, not based on individual logic, but on the search for balance and belonging within the family system as a whole. When a system member is excluded, wronged, or forgotten, the field registers this imbalance and, over time, attempts to restore order through the descendants.

Thus, invisible loyalties arise and shape behaviors, leading people towards fates echoing the lives of ancestors with whom they share more than genetic ties—they share an unresolved emotional history. Such dynamics are not driven by conscious will, but by a systemic need for inclusion and reparation, manifesting as tragic repetitions, unconscious sabotage, illnesses, and conflicts seemingly disconnected from personal biography. What at first glance seems like bad luck or individual destiny, through a systemic lens, reveals itself as the expression of an active collective pain seeking recognition and resolution.

The presence of the systemic unconscious compels a profound reassessment of how we understand emotional conflicts, relationship difficulties, and existential impasses. It invites us to broaden the focus of psychological investigation, shifting from looking solely at the personal trajectory to considering the network of intergenerational bonds in which we are embedded. Perceiving that the causes of our suffering may be rooted in events occurring decades before our birth expands our capacity for compassion and understanding—not only for ourselves but for the entire lineage to which we belong. This perspective brings the possibility of reframing pain, interrupting cycles of unconscious repetition, and inaugurating new paths of freedom, where the legacy of those who came before no longer needs to be carried as a burden, but can be integrated with awareness, gratitude, and peace.

If the systemic field is the atmosphere we breathe in our groups of belonging, the systemic unconscious can be thought of as the deep currents and ancestral memories contained within that field. It is a vast collective reservoir, specific to each system, accumulating and preserving the experiences, traumas, secrets, fates, and emotions lived by all members who came before us. It is a dimension transcending individual consciousness and even the explicit memory of current members, yet exerting continuous and sometimes decisive influence over their lives. This concept radically expands our view of the human psyche, revealing that we carry not only our personal history but also an inherited psychic legacy, an invisible inheritance shaping our perceptions, driving our behaviors, and weaving the threads of our destiny in ways often escaping rational comprehension.

The nature of this systemic unconscious differs substantially from the more familiar concept of the personal unconscious, popularized by Freudian psychoanalysis. While the personal unconscious is primarily a repository of repressed contents from individual experience – desires, fears, fantasies, childhood memories pushed out of awareness for being painful or socially unacceptable – the systemic unconscious operates on a transindividual level. It belongs not to a single person, but to the system as a whole. Its "language" is not primarily that of dream symbols or individual slips of the tongue, but that of pattern repetitions, relational entanglements, and emotional resonances crossing generations. The intelligence operating in the systemic unconscious focuses not on the individual's intrapsychic dynamics, but on the group's cohesion and balance (or imbalance). It "remembers" those excluded, "feels" injustices committed, "carries" unlived griefs, and "seeks" compensation for past disorders, using current members as vehicles for expression, often without their having any notion of what is happening on a deeper level. It is a relational intelligence, oriented towards the dynamics of belonging and order within the larger field.

The way the systemic unconscious exerts its influence is predominantly silent and hidden. Descendants are affected by this collective memory field without needing to know the stories or the people involved. Transmission occurs not through explicit narratives, but via a kind of energetic and emotional resonance. An individual might feel inexplicably drawn to a partner who makes them relive a suffering dynamic similar to their grandparents'. Another might develop a paralyzing fear of water without ever having a personal traumatic experience, later discovering an ancestor drowned. Someone might feel a diffuse, persistent guilt preventing them from enjoying life, later realizing this guilt echoes that of a family member involved in a tragic event. These connections are established below the threshold of consciousness. The person simply finds themselves repeating a pattern, feeling an emotion, or suffering from a symptom that seems to lack logical explanation in their own biography. It's as if they are responding to an invisible call, a deep loyalty to the system, enacting a drama that did not begin with them. This unconscious repetition of patterns is the hallmark of the systemic unconscious in action, the system's blind attempt to bring to light what remained hidden or unresolved.

Understanding the existence and workings of the systemic unconscious offers us a fundamental key to deciphering many of the most challenging aspects of our lives. How many of us struggle against self-destructive behaviors that seem to have a will of their own? How many experience fears or anxieties paralyzing us without apparent cause? How many find ourselves stuck in unsatisfying relationships repeating a painful script? How many suffer from chronic illnesses that traditional medicine struggles to fully explain or alleviate? The systemic perspective invites us to consider the possibility that the roots of much of this suffering are located not only in our childhood or conscious choices, but extend back to the untold stories and unhealed wounds of our ancestors, whose echoes still resonate in the systemic unconscious we share. This understanding seeks not to diminish the importance of personal history or individual responsibility, but rather to add a crucial layer of understanding. Recognizing that we might be entangled in transgenerational dynamics allows space for deeper compassion for ourselves and our challenges, and also for the possibility of seeking solutions beyond the purely individual level.

But how can we access this hidden dimension? If the systemic unconscious operates outside our usual perception, how can we become aware of its influences? The answer lies in attentive observation of repeating patterns. The systemic unconscious, though silent, leaves visible traces in our lives and family histories.

Repetitions are its signature. We must become detectives of our own history and our clan's history, looking for recurring themes. Are there repeating relationship patterns (betrayals, abandonments, unhappy marriages)? Are certain types of illnesses or accidents more frequent in some lineages? Are there critical ages where significant events (positive or negative) tend to occur? Are there repeating professions, financial difficulties, or migration patterns? Are there names, birth dates, or death dates that coincide strikingly? The occurrence of similar fates across different generations (addictions, depression, suicide, unexplained success or failure) strongly indicates the operation of a systemic entanglement. By mapping these repetitions, without judgment but with investigative curiosity, we begin to outline the contours of themes and loyalties active in our family's systemic unconscious. This attentive observation of facts and patterns is the main gateway to this hidden dimension, allowing what was unconscious to begin emerging into the light of consciousness.

The concept of the systemic unconscious confronts us with the reality that we are much more than isolated individuals. We are links in a long chain of generations, bearers of a complex psychic heritage, woven with threads of joys, pains, challenges, and achievements of those who came before us. Recognizing the existence of this collective memory field and learning to decipher its language through repetitions is a journey of profound consciousness expansion. It frees us from the illusion that we are entirely authors of our own destiny, while simultaneously returning to us the responsibility to consciously deal with the legacy we received. By understanding the transgenerational roots of some of our suffering, we can begin to disidentify from them, symbolically return burdens not belonging to us, and honor our ancestors in a way that allows us to follow our own path with more freedom and integrity. The systemic unconscious is not an immutable burden, but a field of potentialities transformable by the light of consciousness and the movement of reconciliation and inclusion.

Chapter 7
Physics and Consciousness

The understanding of reality as a participatory construction gains strength as knowledge advances beyond purely objective observation, revealing a deep interdependence between the observing subject and the observed phenomenon. Human consciousness, far from being an isolated function within an organism, begins to be recognized as an integral part of a vaster field where mind, matter, and energy interact dynamically and subtly. This new reading of the world rests not only on philosophical or spiritual interpretations but finds support in contemporary scientific discoveries challenging the fragmented and reductionist view of reality, paving the way for a systemic perception encompassing both the visible and invisible, the tangible and intuitive.

The progress of complexity sciences and modern physics, especially through quantum theory, has brought forth a scenario where boundaries between observer and phenomenon become increasingly blurred. The mechanistic paradigm, guiding our understanding of the universe for centuries, yields to an approach where the whole is more than the sum of its parts, and where interactions, contexts, and fields of influence play determining roles in event manifestation. In this scenario, consciousness ceases being an isolated epiphenomenon of brain activity and starts being considered an agent capable of interacting with the very fabric of reality, shaping possibilities and acting as co-author of lived experiences. This understanding inaugurates a new way of positioning ourselves before the world and ourselves, shifting us from passive spectators to active participants in the reality creation process. The quality of presence, the intention guiding our actions, the emotional patterns we sustain, and even the bonds we nurture within the systems we belong to are recognized as factors concretely influencing the paths opening or closing before us. Thus emerges an ethics of attention and responsibility, where each conscious gesture resonates beyond the individual, reverberating in the collective field and contributing to weaving a world that is both reflection and extension of our deepest consciousness.

For centuries, the predominant worldview in the West was marked by Cartesian dualism – a strict separation between mind and matter, observer and observed – and by mechanistic physics describing the universe as a large, predictable machine composed of separate parts. However, the scientific revolutions of the 20th century, especially the advent of quantum physics, profoundly shook these pillars, suggesting a reality much stranger, interconnected, and, surprisingly, participatory. This chapter does not intend to be a physics course, but rather to explore some disconcerting notions emerging from this field and how they resonate with the systemic perspective and the idea that consciousness plays an active role in constructing the world we experience.

Quantum physics, investigating the realm of the very small – atoms and subatomic particles – encountered phenomena completely challenging our intuition based on the macroscopic world. One such phenomenon is non-locality, exemplified by the concept of quantum entanglement. Two particles that once interacted can remain connected such that an action performed on one instantly affects the other, no matter the distance separating them. This "spooky action at a distance," as Einstein skeptically called it, suggests a fundamental interconnection in the fabric of reality, an underlying unity transcending classical notions of space and time. For the systemic perspective, this idea finds a powerful echo in observing how family or group members can remain connected and mutually influence each other profoundly, even when physically distant or belonging to different generations, as if linked by invisible threads within a shared field.

Another intriguing quantum concept is the collapse of the wave function. Before being measured or observed, quantum systems seem to exist in a state of superposition, a cloud of potentialities described by a mathematical wave function. Only at the moment of observation or interaction with a measuring instrument (or, some argue, with consciousness) does this cloud of possibilities "collapse," and the system assumes a definite state, manifesting as a particle with specific properties at a certain location. This discovery raised profound questions about the observer's role in creating observed reality. Is reality "out there" something fixed and independent, or does it only define and manifest itself in relation to a conscious observer? Although the exact interpretation of these phenomena is still intensely debated among physicists, the implication strongly resonating with many spiritual traditions and depth psychology is that consciousness is not a mere passive spectator of the universe, but an active participant in its unfolding.

This possibility of active consciousness in reality manifestation has been explored by various thinkers navigating the interface between science, philosophy, and spirituality. Physicist Amit Goswami, for example, advocates a worldview based on "monistic idealism," where consciousness is the primary reality, the foundation of all being, and matter is a manifestation within consciousness. David Bohm, physicist and Einstein collaborator, proposed a model of reality as an undivided whole in motion ("holomovement"), with an implicit order (an unmanifest potential, similar to the quantum field) and an explicit order (the world we perceive). For Bohm, our fragmented perception of reality is an illusion obscuring this underlying totality. Deepak Chopra, physician and writer, has been a prominent popularizer of ideas about mind-body connection and consciousness's potential to influence health and well-being, drawing on interpretations of quantum physics and Vedic wisdom. Although the approaches of these and other authors vary, they share a vision challenging strict materialism and pointing towards a universe where mind and matter are intrinsically interconnected.

If we accept, even as a hypothesis or powerful metaphor, that consciousness plays an active role in how reality presents itself to us, this has direct implications for our daily lives. It suggests that the quality of our attention and the clarity of our intention are tools of considerable power. Where we place our focus – on problems or solutions, fear or trust, scarcity or abundance – seems to influence not only our subjective perception but also the experiences and opportunities we encounter. Focused and sustained attention acts like a beam of light illuminating certain possibilities in the vast field of potential, while intention, when charged with feeling and clarity of purpose, acts as a directing force mobilizing internal and external energies towards a goal. This does not mean simplistic magical thinking, where merely wishing for something makes it happen, but rather recognizing that our inner landscape – thoughts, emotions, beliefs, intentions – creates a resonance field interacting with the larger field of reality, shaping how we experience it and the responses we get from the world. Reality, in this sense, is not just something that happens to us, but something in whose creation we actively participate through the quality of our consciousness.

Now, how can we connect these seemingly abstract ideas with Systemic Psychology and the concrete dynamics of human relationships? The bridge becomes clear when considering that we rarely exist in a vacuum of individual consciousness. We are constantly immersed in fields of shared consciousness – the systemic fields of our families, work groups, communities. If individual consciousness can act as a factor in reality manifestation, then a system's collective consciousness, with its shared beliefs, predominant emotions, and intentions (often unconscious), must be an even more potent force. The bonds uniting us are not just social or emotional structures; they also function as channels and fields of energetic and informational interference. Invisible loyalties, family secrets, implicit expectations, unspoken system "rules" – all create a specific consciousness field influencing the perception and behavior of all its members. This field can facilitate certain outcomes and hinder others, creating recurring patterns defining the "reality" of that specific system. Our bonds, therefore, are not just part of our life experience; they are active agents in co-creating that experience, functioning as lenses and force fields shaping what is possible or probable for us within that relational context. Changing our individual reality often requires not only inner work but also a change in the quality of our bonds and the dynamics of the systemic field we belong to.

Exploring these connections between physics, consciousness, and systemic psychology invites us to adopt a more integrated and participatory worldview. Rigid boundaries between observer and observed, inner and outer, begin to dissolve. We recognize ourselves not as isolated gears in a universal machine, nor as passive victims of circumstances or family heritage, but as interconnected centers of consciousness, endowed with the capacity to influence and co-create reality through the quality of our presence, attention, intention, and, fundamentally, the quality of our relationships. This perception brings a deep sense of responsibility, as every thought, feeling, and interaction contributes to the collective web of existence. It also brings immense potential for freedom and transformation, showing us that by cultivating our consciousness and working to heal and harmonize our bonds, we can actively participate in creating a reality more aligned with our deepest values and the well-being of the whole.

Chapter 8
Collective Reality

Human reality is, in essence, an intersubjective phenomenon, continuously woven in interactions between individuals and the social systems they belong to. From the first moments of life, each human being is inserted into a pre-existing symbolic and relational environment, composed of languages, myths, institutions, and power structures influencing, guiding, and often defining their possibilities of being and acting. Birth represents not only the start of biological existence but entry into a collective universe laden with historically constructed meanings. This early immersion in a shared field of representations and norms shapes reality perception, delineating contours of what is understood as possible, acceptable, or true. Thus, daily experience emerges not exclusively from individual perception, but from the constant intertwining of subjectivity and the cultural matrices permeating social life.

The constitution of the lived world thus occurs from tacit and explicit agreements established over generations. These agreements, even when invisible or seemingly natural, sustain a collective way of perceiving, interpreting, and responding to reality. They are symbolic pacts underpinning institutions, organizing interpersonal relations, and structuring expectations about social roles, human destiny, and the meaning of existence. By internalizing these cultural codes, we almost automatically reproduce patterns governing the collectivity. Belonging to a group, far from being neutral, involves assimilating a symbolic repertoire guiding both our beliefs and deepest emotions. And as this repertoire is shared by a critical mass of people, it acquires a shaping force conferring upon collective reality the character of objective truth, even if this truth is just one among many possible world constructions.

This collective field acts as a consciousness-forming matrix, serving simultaneously as ground and limit for subjective experience. Language, rituals, educational and religious systems, symbols, and media narratives operate as vehicles of this matrix, continuously transmitting fundamentals of what is perceived as real. This field's strength lies not only in its elements' coherence but in its capacity to generate a sense of normality rarely questioned. It is in this consensual environment that human dramas unfold, identities are constructed, and individual dreams are projected. Understanding this dynamic is fundamental for any journey of self-knowledge and transformation, for only by recognizing the collective roots of perceived reality can one begin to question, reformulate, and ultimately transcend limits imposed by tradition, culture, and dominant belief systems.

We now enter the vast territory of collective reality, the complex tapestry of shared beliefs, values, norms, behaviors, and bonds characterizing larger human groups – cultures, societies, nations, and even humanity as a whole. The fundamental premise we explore here is that the "reality" most of us experience daily is largely a co-creation of these collective systems. It's not a neutral perception of an objective world, but an interpretation deeply shaped by the implicit and explicit agreements governing the groups we belong to.

This co-creation of collective reality occurs through multiple interconnected mechanisms. The language we speak, for example, is not just a means of communication; it structures our thought, categorizes our experience, and carries a universe of cultural assumptions. Institutions organizing our social life – schools, governments, legal systems, economic markets, religious organizations – establish rules, define roles, and distribute power, shaping our opportunities and expectations. Cultural narratives, conveyed through media, education, art, and traditions, offer models of how we should be, feel, and act, defining what is considered "normal," "successful," or "desirable". Deeply ingrained beliefs about human nature, life's purpose, right and wrong, sacred and profane, permeate the social fabric and are absorbed by us, often unquestioningly, from the earliest age. The result is a "consensual reality," a set of shared understandings allowing us to function in society, but which, simultaneously, can limit our perception of the vast possibilities existing beyond this consensus. We take this social construction as reality itself, forgetting it is essentially a collective agreement, amenable to change and transformation.

It is crucial to recognize we are affected not only by our personal history and family-of-origin dynamics but also by these broader sociocultural and spiritual patterns traversing us. Our gender identity, social class, ethnic origin, nationality – all these categories place us within specific collective systems, each with its own histories, privileges, oppressions, and expectations. We often carry, unknowingly, marks of collective historical traumas, like wars, colonization, slavery, or persecutions, which left scars on social systems and continue influencing intergroup relations and individual opportunities in the present. Similarly, we are permeated by spiritual and philosophical currents predominant in our culture, shaping our views on life's meaning, death, ethics, and our relationship with the transcendent. These larger patterns operate as invisible force fields, influencing our choices, relationships, and sense of belonging or alienation in the world, going far beyond purely familial dynamics. Ignoring these collective influences means missing a fundamental piece of the puzzle of who we are.

We can understand the manifestation of these collective patterns through the lens of the collective unconscious, a concept suggesting a deep psychic layer, shared by all humanity or large cultural groups, containing archetypes, symbols, and ancestral memories. This collective unconscious is not an abstract entity; it expresses itself concretely in the structures and dynamics of our social life. A culture's founding myths, legends and fairy tales, rites of passage, seasonal celebrations – all are symbolic expressions of universal archetypes and themes. Social roles we play (father, mother, child, professional, leader, follower) often reflect archetypal behavior and relationship patterns. Our families, as microcosms of society, become arenas where these great themes of the collective unconscious are enacted and transmitted. Power struggles, patterns of love and betrayal, sacrifices, and quests for meaning seen in our families echo much older and universal narratives. By playing our familial and social roles, we are often unknowingly participating in the continuous representation of these collective dramas, perpetuating beliefs and behaviors inherited through countless generations.

Faced with this realization – that we are immersed in constructed collective realities and permeated by inherited unconscious patterns – an essential invitation arises for those seeking self-knowledge and spiritual freedom: the exercise of discernment. We must begin to question, honestly and courageously, the "truths" we take for granted. Which of my beliefs about success, happiness, relationships, money, body, health, spirituality are genuinely mine, born from my experience and reflection, and which were simply absorbed from my familial, social, cultural, or religious environment? Which fears I carry are responses to real and present dangers, and which are echoes of collective anxieties or historical traumas? Which social roles do I play automatically, without questioning if they truly correspond to my essence and purpose? This investigation process requires attentive observation of our own thoughts, feelings, and behaviors, and also a critical look at the messages and expectations received from the systems we belong to. It's not about rejecting everything outright, but developing the ability to separate the wheat from the chaff, identify inherited constructions limiting us, and recognize those nurturing and supporting us.

This act of discernment and disidentification from limiting collective constructions is profoundly liberating. Realizing that many "walls" seemingly confining our reality are actually inherited mental and social constructs gives us the key to transcend them. Awareness that a limiting belief is not an absolute truth, but a cultural or familial product, empowers us to question it, choose not to feed it anymore, and open space for new perspectives. When we recognize a social role we play no longer serves us or doesn't reflect who we truly are, we can begin moving out of it, seeking more authentic forms of expression and contribution. This awareness does not isolate us from the collective; on the contrary, it allows us to participate more consciously and intentionally. We can choose which values and worldviews we want to strengthen and which collective narratives we want to help transform. Opening space for a new reality begins with the courage to question inherited consensual reality and the willingness to listen to the deeper voice of our own soul, which often whispers possibilities collective systems do not yet recognize. By doing so, we not only transform our own experience but also contribute to the evolution of collective consciousness as a whole.

Chapter 9
Systemic Health

Human health cannot be fully understood when isolated from its relational, historical, and energetic context. It emerges as an integrated expression of numerous factors transcending purely physiological or psychological dimensions. Instead of just being a static state of clinical normality, health reveals itself as a dynamic manifestation of balance between the individual and the multiple systems they are part of. The body, mind, emotions, interpersonal relationships, family bonds, and even transgenerational influences compose a living, interdependent ecosystem shaping our well-being. Within this expanded perspective, there is no isolated "I" from "us"; the vitality we experience is directly proportional to the harmony we establish with the flows of belonging, exchange, and recognition within the systems surrounding us.

This broader understanding of health demands a profound paradigm shift. Purely causal analysis centered on pathogens, genetic flaws, or individual mental disorders becomes limited before the systemic complexity characterizing human existence. Emotional experiences, inherited behavior patterns, unconscious loyalties to family members, exclusions remaining silenced in past generations – all influence the state of balance or imbalance often manifesting through physical symptoms. Health, in this sense, becomes a subtle dance between the visible and invisible, between what is directly felt and what is transmitted through non-conscious relational fields. Each human organism carries a living memory of the bonds constituting it, and this memory continuously expresses itself in the body, mood, affects, and how each person positions themselves in life.

The body is not just where health reveals itself or illness settles – it is the direct mirror of the network of belongings and meanings sustaining each human being's existence. When something in a family system remains unresolved, forgotten, or excluded, this imbalance may find expression in a later system member. This expression can take the form of a physical symptom, a repetitive pattern of suffering, or a persistent feeling of disconnection from life. In this context, health is not just an individual asset, but a reflection of order, inclusion, and clarity in systemic bonds. Cultivating health thus means restoring bond order, recognizing difficult fates, freeing oneself from unconscious loyalties, and creating space for life to flow with more authenticity, lightness, and freedom.

The systemic perspective, however, invites us to radically broaden this view, introducing the concept of Systemic Health. Under this lens, health transcends the mere absence of diagnosable symptoms; it emerges as a dynamic state of balance, a fluid harmony manifesting in the constant interaction between our relational bonds, personal and transgenerational history, emotional patterns, and individual energy field. We are not isolated units whose health depends only on internal factors, but interconnected beings whose vitality reflects the quality and balance of the systems we belong to.

Defining systemic health implies recognizing this complex interdependence. It flourishes when there is satisfactory balance on several fronts simultaneously. Firstly, in bonds: feeling belonging, occupying one's place with dignity within the family and other significant groups, maintaining relationships with a reasonable flow of exchange and mutual respect are crucial factors. Relationships marked by exclusions, chronic conflicts, hierarchical inversions, or severe imbalances in giving and receiving tend to undermine life force. Secondly, health depends on integrating personal and transgenerational history: it's the ability to look at one's biography and family legacy with clarity and acceptance, recognizing both wounds and resources, without being trapped in unconscious repetitions or blind loyalties to difficult fates. Denying or fighting against one's history drains energy. Thirdly, we consider emotional patterns: systemic health involves the capacity to feel, express, and process emotions fluidly and appropriately to the context, differentiating feelings genuinely ours from those possibly echoing unresolved emotions in the family field. Chronic repression or identification with systemic emotions can generate tensions manifesting in the body. Finally, all this reflects in the individual's energy field: a sense of vitality, flow, purpose, and connection to life. When bonds are in order, history is integrated, and emotions flow, vital energy circulates more freely, sustaining health on all levels.

If systemic health is this state of dynamic balance, illness or symptoms, in turn, can be understood as signs that this balance has been disturbed at some system level. The systemic perspective teaches us to look beyond the individual physical or psychological manifestation and investigate potential underlying relational disorders. Often, illness arises as the system's attempt to bring to light something hidden, excluded, or disrespected. An illness might be the physical expression of a profound violation of the Orders of Love: perhaps a family member is unconsciously representing an excluded ancestor, "falling ill" in their place so they are remembered; perhaps a child develops symptoms trying to "save" the parents' marriage, diverting attention to themselves; perhaps physical burnout results from a chronic imbalance in giving and receiving in a professional or affective relationship. In other cases, the symptom might manifest a deep identification with an ancestor's fate, where the person, out of blind love, repeats an illness or suffering pattern as loyalty. Illness, in this context, ceases being seen merely as individual misfortune to become a complex message, a call from the system to look at a deeper wound crying for recognition and healing.

In this dynamic, the physical body assumes a crucial role as spokesperson for what cannot be said or processed on other levels. The body does not lie. It registers relational tensions, absorbs unexpressed emotions, and manifests hidden conflicts in the system. Chronic pains, digestive problems, autoimmune diseases, allergies, sleep disorders, skin conditions – many symptoms, while potentially having biomedical components, often also carry systemic meaning. They might be metaphors for an unsustainable relational situation (back pain reflecting the burden of carrying responsibilities not one's own), somatization of "frozen" emotions (neck stiffness linked to unexpressed anger), or physical representation of a family secret (vision problems related to something the family "doesn't want to see"). When the individual psyche and the system's collective dynamic fail to process certain experiences or acknowledge certain truths, the body often takes on the task of expressing them, through the language of symptoms. Listening to the body with this systemic perspective opens a communication channel to the deepest layers of our personal and family history.

Therefore, the systemic approach invites us to radically broaden our view of symptoms. Instead of seeing them merely as enemies to fight or flaws to correct, we are encouraged to relate to them with curiosity and respect, as potential messengers. Faced with a physical symptom or psychic suffering, we can ask not only "What is the medical diagnosis?" or "What personal trauma might be related?" but also questions like: "What does this symptom prevent me from doing or force me to do? How does it affect my relationships?", "If this symptom could speak, what would it say about my family or history?", "Is there anyone in my family who had a similar fate or was excluded whom I might be representing?", "Is there any significant imbalance in my current life, an area where I give too much or receive too little?". These questions open new avenues for investigation and understanding, allowing us to see the body not as a separate entity, but as a sensitive seismograph, deeply connected to the network of relationships and the history constituting us. Understanding the body as part of an interconnected whole is fundamental for a more integral approach to health.

Finally, this perspective redefines the healing process itself. If illness can manifest a systemic disorder, deep healing rarely comes solely from interventions focused exclusively on the individual symptom. Systemic healing involves a movement back to order, restoration of balance, and, fundamentally, reconnection. It involves recognizing hidden dynamics contributing to the symptom, giving proper place to all system members (including excluded or forgotten ones), honoring hierarchy and the appropriate flow of giving and receiving, and re-establishing a conscious, respectful connection with one's roots and the life force flowing through generations. Often, the simple act of bringing a family secret to light, acknowledging an excluded ancestor, or assuming one's proper place in the correct order can bring surprising relief to persistent symptoms. Healing, in this sense, is not just pain elimination, but restoring flow and belonging within the systemic network. It's a process inviting us to look beyond ourselves and reconnect with the greater wisdom residing in our bonds and shared history.

Chapter 10
Systemic Diagnosis

The practical application of Systemic Psychology demands a profound shift in how we perceive symptoms and conflicts emerging in our lives. Understanding that the individual is inseparable from the relational field they belong to decisively broadens our view on human suffering and transformation. Instead of seeking isolated explanations located in individual biography or purely internal factors, we are called to perceive an invisible network of bonds, loyalties, repetitions, and exclusions shaping behaviors, emotions, and destinies. This approach not only enriches understanding of human difficulties but also points to broader, more effective paths for resolving impasses that initially seem purely personal. We enter territory where sensitive listening to the symptom reveals its own language: the language of the family system and its hidden dynamics.

This new way of seeing brings transformative implications. The systemic gaze leads us to investigate not "what is wrong" with someone, but rather "what needs to be seen" in that system. It invites us to consider that recurring symptoms, existential blockages, illnesses, or failures might be fulfilling specific functions within a larger plot involving not just the present, but also past events and bonds still influencing the present. This reading rests on the idea that the system constantly seeks balance, albeit in painful ways, and that invisible orders exist which, when violated, generate disconnection and suffering. Thus, systemic diagnosis configures as deep listening to the relational field, sensitive to bond subtleties and messages behind apparent chaos.

For this, a new quality of attention is needed—perception trained not just for what is said, but also for what is omitted, for family silences, excluded fates, and surprisingly precise repeating patterns. It's an exercise in presence demanding openness, humility, and willingness to abandon reductionist explanations. This type of listening goes beyond behavioral surfaces and accesses deeper layers of being, where often reside both unprocessed trauma and the life force seeking expression. Systemic diagnosis, therefore, is not a classification tool, but an instrument of consciousness. It allows us to recognize dynamics imprisoning us and, by doing so, opens the possibility to reposition ourselves more freely, maturely, and integratedly within the system we belong to.

We begin this practical phase with the theme of Systemic Diagnosis, a concept here acquiring a meaning distinct from that usually employed in traditional medical or psychological contexts. It's not about assigning labels or classifying individual pathologies, but rather developing a keen perceptual capacity, a "systemic lens" allowing us to see hidden relational dynamics, transgenerational patterns, and violations of fundamental orders often underlying emotional, physical, or behavioral symptoms afflicting us.

The first and most crucial change proposed by systemic diagnosis is the radical broadening of focus. Instead of concentrating investigation exclusively on the individual presenting the symptom or difficulty, the systemic perspective invites us to look at the broader relational context. The individual is seen not as the isolated origin of the problem, but often as the spokesperson, the visible "symptom" of an imbalance or unresolved issue in the larger system they belong to – primarily, the family of origin and current family, but also other relevant systems. Therefore, a genuine systemic diagnosis never limits itself to the person; it seeks to understand the symptom in light of family history, invisible loyalties, unspoken secrets, occurred exclusions, and how the orders of love (belonging, hierarchy, balance) are being respected or violated in that specific system. The fundamental question shifts from "What is wrong with this person?" to "What is this symptom revealing about this system's dynamic?".

To develop this systemic lens, we need to train our observation to identify certain key patterns and elements often signaling hidden dynamics. One of the most evident indicators is repetitive patterns. As mentioned, the systemic unconscious tends to manifest through repetitions. We must investigate: what themes, events, relationship types, illnesses, accidents, successes, or failures repeat across generations in our family? At what ages or life stages do certain significant events tend to occur? What patterns in our own lives seem to echo stories of our parents, grandparents, or other relatives? Clearly identifying a repetition strongly indicates an active systemic theme seeking recognition or resolution.

Another crucial observation focus is family exclusions. The first order of love teaches us everyone has the right to belong. When someone is excluded – whether by premature death and unprocessed grief, abortion, having a fate considered shameful (prison, mental illness, suicide), being a disrespected previous partner, or simply being "forgotten" – the system seeks compensation. Systemic diagnosis involves actively investigating these exclusions. Who is missing from the family story? Who isn't talked about? What secrets might exist? Often, the person manifesting a symptom today is unconsciously connected to one of these excluded individuals, "representing" them or carrying a burden in their name.

We must also observe the quality of bonds, especially the presence of symbiotic or entangled relationships. Although connection is vital, some bonds can become so fused they impede individuation and autonomy. Children remaining excessively attached to parents (or one parent), couples lacking space for individuality, relationships marked by extreme codependency – all can indicate unconscious loyalties or unresolved needs from previous generations keeping people trapped in relational immaturity patterns. Difficulty in healthy separation is an important diagnostic sign.

Finally, observing inherited or delegated roles within the system is useful. People often unconsciously assume certain roles in family dynamics not corresponding to their essence but serving a function for the system: the "parentified child" caring for parents, the "scapegoat" carrying family shadows, the "patient" keeping the family united around their illness, the "hero" needing to compensate for previous failures, etc. Identifying these repetitive or delegated roles helps understand invisible pressures acting on individuals and limiting their freedom to be.

Beyond attentive observation of these elements, systemic diagnosis benefits from using investigative questions opening perspective beyond the obvious. Faced with persistent difficulty, we can ask: "In service of whom or what might this problem be in my family system?", "If I resolved this issue, whom might I symbolically 'lose' or 'betray'?", "Does this feeling afflicting me seem to belong entirely to my personal history, or does it have a larger, older quality?", "What was my parents'/grandparents' situation when they were my current age?", "What significant event in my family's history might be connected to this theme?", "In what aspect am I disrespecting the order of arrival or the balance between giving and receiving in my relationships?". These questions direct attention towards possible systemic roots of the problem.

Complementarily, certain warning signs can indicate high probability of entanglement: feeling responsible for people or situations not within one's purview; experiencing intense, recurring emotions without apparent cause; feeling diffuse guilt or a sense of not having the right to be happy or successful; repetitive failures despite genuine effort; frequent accidents; chronic or serious illnesses without satisfactory medical explanation; feeling "stuck" or unable to move forward in life.

It is fundamental to reiterate that this diagnosis's purpose is not to label, judge, or find culprits. The goal is understanding. Bringing to light hidden dynamics, invisible loyalties, and violated orders possibly sustaining a symptom or suffering pattern provides clarity on the systemic logic behind the problem. This understanding alone can be profoundly liberating, allowing us to disidentify from the blind pattern and begin envisioning new possibilities for action and positioning within the system. Systemic diagnosis is essentially an act of bringing awareness to what operated in shadows.

This diagnostic practice requires not just technical knowledge, but sensitive, open listening capable of embracing human system complexity without reducing it to simplistic explanations. By illuminating hidden movements operating behind suffering, systemic diagnosis invites us to recognize imbalance not as error, but as the system's attempt to find compensation or balance before old wounds. This transformative listening shifts focus from the "problem" to seeking reconnection with what was excluded, devalued, or forgotten. The therapist, in this context, acts as facilitator of symbolic reconciliations, supporting the client in building new ways of belonging and occupying their place with more lightness and integrity. Over time, this approach broadens the client's own awareness, who begins recognizing echoes of previous stories in their trajectory and understanding their pain as part of something larger—an intergenerational narrative crying for recognition. The person then ceases seeing themselves as "symptom bearer" and begins understanding themselves as a living expression of the system, with the opportunity to interrupt repetitions and reintegrate fragmented bonds. It's at this point diagnosis ceases being an analytical tool to become a lever for transformation: naming hidden dynamics and honoring what needs inclusion creates a new field of possibilities, where more conscious choices can finally emerge.

Ultimately, systemic diagnosis reveals itself as a profound gesture of love towards the system. It seeks no culprits, points no individual flaws, but recognizes the strength and pain contained in movements each member makes in the name of belonging. The clarity achieved with this gaze is, in itself, restorative. It offers the individual the chance to reposition themselves, not against their history, but from it—with more freedom, compassion, and responsibility. In this sense, diagnosing systemically is above all an act of seeing: seeing what was hidden, recognizing what needs inclusion, and allowing life's flow to resume with more harmony.

Chapter 11
Family Constellation

Family Constellation establishes itself as a profoundly transformative approach that allows access to, representation of, and reordering of the hidden dynamics governing human systems, especially families. Its strength lies in the ability to make the invisible visible, offering a faithful mirror of the loyalties, exclusions, role inversions, and other systemic entanglements acting silently across generations. The experiential process provided by this method is not limited to external observation; it calls the person to dive into a deeper truth manifesting bodily and emotionally in the relational field. By highlighting the unconscious forces shaping repetitive patterns of suffering, Family Constellation presents itself not just as a therapeutic tool, but as an invitation to recognition and reconciliation with one's own history, ancestral roots, and the vital flow manifesting through bonds of belonging.

At the heart of this work lies the principle that we all carry, often unknowingly, fragments of our ancestors' emotional history – stories of loss, trauma, exclusions, and disorders that, when unrecognized, perpetuate themselves as symptoms, blockages, or difficult fates.

Constellation acts as a revealing lens, dismantling the rational explanations we often use to justify our dilemmas and staging a broader truth involving entire generations. A person participating in a constellation contacts this larger dimension, transcending individual biography and accessing an interconnected information field. This field, by its phenomenological nature, allows symbolic representations – whether people or objects – to capture and express with impressive accuracy the tensions, pains, and interrupted movements present in the system. Recognizing these dynamics, combined with small gestures of inclusion, honor, or symbolic return of undue burdens, can trigger subtle yet profoundly liberating movements.

More than a technique, Family Constellation is an experience of presence and listening to what lies beyond the apparent. It operates through a non-verbal, silent, and sensitive language, communicating through the body and emotions, allowing information contained in a system's collective unconscious to reveal itself spontaneously. This revelation aims not just for understanding, but for restoring balance and order in affective and transgenerational relationships. By touching such deep layers of human existence, constellation promotes an expansion of consciousness that often positively impacts various life areas. With this, it becomes possible to transform rigid patterns into new relationship possibilities, assuming one's place in the system with dignity and lightness. Family Constellation, therefore, not only illuminates the path of self-knowledge but also paves a trail of healing extending beyond the individual, reaching the invisible fabric of preceding and future generations.

Family Constellations operate on the same fundamental principles explored earlier, the Orders of Love: the inalienable right to belong, the importance of hierarchy based on order of arrival, and the need for balance in exchanges between giving and receiving. The method starts from the premise that many of our current problems – be they relationship difficulties, health issues, financial problems, or existential blockages – have roots in violations of these orders occurring in our family system, often in past generations. Hellinger's genius was discovering a way to make these invisible dynamics visible, using a fascinating phenomenon occurring when a spatial representation of the family system in question is created.

The heart of Family Constellation lies in accessing a phenomenon Hellinger called the "knowing field" or phenomenological field. When, in a workshop or session, a person (the client) wishes to look at an issue and chooses others (representatives) to position themselves in the space representing family members (or abstract elements like illness, success, a country), something extraordinary happens. These representatives, even without prior information about the people or situation they represent, often begin experiencing physical sensations, emotions, thoughts, or movement impulses that are not their own, but correspond remarkably accurately to the internal reality or situation of the people represented. It's as if, upon entering the constellation field, they become "antennas" capable of tuning into and expressing relevant information from that family's systemic unconscious. This phenomenon of representative perception, though still mysterious in its exact mechanisms, is the basis allowing the facilitator and client to observe hidden dynamics in action.

Through the spatial arrangement of representatives and their perceptions and interactions, Family Constellation reveals the underlying structure of the problem. We can "see" who is excluded from the system and how this exclusion affects current members; we can perceive where hierarchy has been inverted, with children carrying burdens belonging to parents; we can feel the imbalance in giving and receiving in a relationship; we can identify invisible loyalties binding someone to an ancestor's tragic fate; we can understand the systemic origin of an illness or a pattern of repetitive failure. The constellation offers not intellectual explanations, but a living image, a felt experience of the dynamic. Often, simply visualizing the system's configuration brings profound insight and the beginning of change for the client. The facilitator, guided by their perception of the field and systemic principles, can then intervene minimally, suggesting movements or phrases of recognition and reconciliation that help restore order and allow love to flow healthily again.

Although the best-known format is the group constellation, where real people act as representatives, the methodology can be applied in various ways. In individual constellation, work occurs only between therapist and client. Instead of people, dolls (like Playmobil figures), symbolic objects, pieces of paper, or floor cushions ("floor anchors") are used to represent system members. The client might be invited to move between positions, feeling different perspectives, or the therapist might describe perceived dynamics through object configuration and field resonance. Although the visual dynamic differs, access to the informational field and the possibility of solution movements are equally effective. There is also the possibility of a self-applied or inner constellation, where the person uses systemic principles and their own bodily and intuitive perception to explore issues internally, through visualization exercises or guided meditation. Although requiring more training in subtle perception, this modality allows for continuous self-observation and integration of systemic dynamics in daily life.

One of the most liberating aspects of Family Constellation is its ability to go beyond the rational mind. Our conscious mind operates based on narratives, beliefs, justifications, and defense mechanisms that often prevent us from seeing the deeper truth of our relational dynamics. We try to explain our problems based on our known biography, psychological theories, or moral judgments, but frequently the systemic root remains hidden. Constellation bypasses these mental barriers by directly accessing information contained in the field, expressed through the body, sensations, and movements of representatives (or objects/visualizations). Solutions emerging in a constellation – a phrase of recognition said to an ancestor, a gesture of reverence to parents, inclusion of an excluded member – might not make immediate logical sense but resonate on a deep soul level, bringing a sense of peace, relief, and correction. It's work that dialogues with a greater wisdom, operating according to laws different from those of the everyday mind.

Finally, it's essential to understand that Family Constellation is not merely a diagnostic tool, but a powerful catalyst for reconnection and healing. By revealing entanglements and disorders, it creates the opportunity for resolution movements to happen. Recognizing an excluded one, returning a burden not belonging to us, honoring who came before, finding our correct place in the system – these are movements restoring the Orders of Love and allowing life force, previously blocked or diverted, to flow again through us and our relationships. Constellation helps transform blind love, which bound us to difficult fates out of unconscious loyalty, into conscious love, honoring the past without needing to repeat it. It reconnects us with our roots healthily, allowing us to receive strength from ancestors without carrying their suffering. In this sense, Family Constellation presents itself as a privileged portal for accessing the wisdom of the systemic unconscious and initiating a profound process of healing and liberation, realigning us with the greater flow of life.

Chapter 12
Presence and Intention

The capacity for profound transformation in systemic work resides not exclusively in the techniques used, but in the intimate and silent vibration of those willing to look at the dynamics governing human systems. Presence and Intention are not abstract or peripheral concepts within this approach, but rather the structuring elements defining the depth and integrity of the opening field. Without genuine presence, there is no real contact; without clear and disinterested intention, there is no safe space for truth to surface. The systemic field, by its sensitive and interactive nature, responds not just to what is done, but primarily to how one is being at the moment of interaction. Thus, the quality of being precedes action and sustains any possibility of perception or healing. It is in this vibrant stillness of one available in service to life, without seeking to control or impose solutions, that the true transformative power of systemic work is revealed.

Presence manifests as a state of integral availability, where body, mind, and heart align with the present moment with openness and acceptance. It is not a passive posture, but an attentive and receptive watchfulness, welcoming what manifests without rushing to resolve or judge. This full presence requires inner emptiness – the temporary suspension of personal narratives, expectations, and hidden intentions. By achieving this state of embodied presence, the facilitator or practitioner becomes an anchoring point in the field, allowing the system to reorganize around a clear and neutral center of consciousness. This quality of presence sustains deep listening and allows contact with the subtlest information, inaccessible through logical analysis or the will to help. In real presence, the system feels seen and respected, which in itself constitutes a healing movement.

Intention, in turn, operates as the ethical and energetic compass guiding the entire process. It defines the direction of attention and establishes the relational field's vibration. When intention is rooted in the sincere desire to serve reconciliation, inclusion, and restoration of order, it acts as a clarifier, dissipating ego noises and creating space for the system's wisdom to manifest. However, when intention is contaminated by unconscious needs – like the desire for validation, rush for results, or impulse to "save" the other – it distorts the field and blocks life's natural movement. Thus, more than wanting to help, cultivating an internal state of reverence and humility is necessary, recognizing we do not lead the process, but are led by something greater, expressing itself through the systemic field when there is space, respect, and listening.

Presence and Intention, therefore, are embodied spiritual practices, demanding continuous commitment to one's own self-knowledge process. They are virtues cultivated with discipline and honesty, becoming the very instrument through which the field reveals and reorganizes itself. There are no shortcuts to their achievement, only the path of constant practice, self-observation, and trusting surrender to the mystery inhabiting human systems. When these qualities are present, systemic work transcends technique and becomes a sacred encounter between consciousnesses, a space where life can finally flow freely.

Recalling previous discussions, we understand the systemic field is a living entity, a shared consciousness field demonstrating remarkable sensitivity to the observing consciousness. It is not an inert object coldly analyzed, but a resonance field responding to the vibrational quality of whoever interacts with it. This means the practitioner's, therapist's, or even the person seeking to understand their own family dynamics through self-observation's internal state inevitably influences the field. Our unspoken expectations, unconscious fears, moral judgments, personal needs for recognition or "saving" others – all act as noise, interference potentially obscuring clear perception of real dynamics and even preventing the field's natural movement towards solution. Recognizing this mutual influence between observer and observed field is the first step in cultivating the immense responsibility accompanying any foray into systemic territory.

Given this field sensitivity, what then are the essential internal qualities we need to cultivate to interact respectfully and facilitatively? The first and perhaps most fundamental is Full Presence. Being present, in this context, goes far beyond simply being physically in the same place. It refers to a state of consciousness anchored in the here and now, with focused attention, open senses, and deep connection to one's body. It's a state of centeredness, of being "at home" within oneself, free from past distractions or future anxieties. This embodied presence creates a field of stability and safety allowing the system's subtle information – sensations, emotions, images, movements – to emerge and be perceived without distortion. Without this quality of presence, we risk projecting our own issues onto the field or missing the delicate signals it offers.

Intimately linked to presence is the quality of Non-Judgment. To perceive a system's reality as it is, we need to radically suspend our personal filters of moral judgment, opinions about right or wrong, good or bad, just or unjust regarding the fates and behaviors of that system's members. The systemic field operates according to its own laws – the Orders of Love – often challenging our conventional moral logic. Attempting to impose our own values or take sides in systemic conflicts only entangles us further and blocks the possibility of a solution serving the whole. The non-judgmental stance requires deep humility and capacity to accept reality as it presents itself, even when painful or difficult to understand. It means looking at all system members with equal respect, recognizing each has their place and fate, and that often the most difficult behaviors stem from blind loyalties or deep entanglements.

The third essential quality is Intention. What purpose moves us when looking at a system or facilitating a process for someone? Intention, in systemic work, should not be to "fix" the system, impose a solution, or alleviate suffering at any cost according to our own will. The most appropriate intention is to serve life, reconciliation, and restoration of order within that specific system, with deep respect for everyone's fate. It's an intention springing from a place of compassionate love, humility, and trust in the field's inherent wisdom. A pure intention, free from the facilitator's ego needs (to be recognized, succeed, control), creates clear, open resonance in the field, allowing healing movements to arise organically. The vibrational quality of our intention – whether loving and respectful or contaminated by fear, judgment, or desire for power – directly affects the work's atmosphere and achievable results.

Cultivating these qualities – full presence, non-judgment, pure intention – is not something happening overnight, but a path of continuous personal and spiritual development. Practices can assist in this cultivation. Inner Silence, sought through meditation, mindfulness, or quiet moments in nature, helps calm the incessant thought flow and create an internal space of clarity and receptivity. Deep Listening practice trains us to hear beyond words, perceive unspoken emotions, bodily messages, significant silences – both in ourselves and others. It's listening involving the whole being, not just ears. And, fundamentally, we need to cultivate Alignment with the Larger Field, developing trust in systemic intelligence and the Orders of Love. This implies letting go of the need to control the process, surrendering to what shows itself, and acting with humility, recognizing we are merely facilitators of a movement greater than us.

This alignment posture leads us to understand our function in systemic work not as protagonist holding answers and directing the scene, but as Channel. Our task is creating and sustaining a safe space, maintaining clear, neutral presence, offering perceptions or pointed interventions serving the field's movement towards order and reconciliation. One must empty oneself, one's theories and desires, to allow the system's wisdom to manifest through us. The cleaner and more unobstructed the channel, the more clearly information can flow and the more effectively the system can find its own reorganization path. This requires courage not to know, endure discomfort of the unresolved, trust the solution emerges from the field itself when appropriate conditions are offered.

Therefore, this chapter represents an invitation to profound inner work, a true training of ethical and energetic consciousness. Proposing to look at systemic dynamics, ours or others', assumes significant responsibility. Clarity about our unresolved issues, integrity of intention, unconditional respect for others' fate are not optional, but fundamental ethical prerequisites. The quality of our presence and purity of intention are safeguards ensuring our intervention serves healing and not entanglement perpetuation. Developing this internal posture is a continuous path of self-knowledge and spiritual refinement, essential for anyone wishing to navigate deep waters of human systems with wisdom, compassion, and effectiveness.

Chapter 13
Quantum Communication

Communication plays a structuring and dynamic role in human relationships, constituting a creative act modeling, sustaining, and transforming interpersonal and systemic bonds. Far beyond a simple data transmission channel, each form of verbal, gestural, or silent expression configures as a concrete manifestation of internal states, emotional intentions, and relational postures. Every time we communicate, we move invisible energy flows traversing relational fields, touching not only the direct interlocutor but reverberating throughout the system we belong to. Human language, therefore, does not operate in isolation; it anchors in deep layers of meaning and vibration, influencing family structures, social groups, and even organizational spaces. What we say—or fail to say—has the power to restore or fragment, welcome or distance, heal or perpetuate old wounds, as our words and attitudes intertwine with the collective's memories and dynamics. Communicating is a gesture of presence, conscious involvement with the other and the whole, demanding more than logic and technical clarity: it requires sensitive inner listening, capable of capturing the impact our messages exert on the common field we share. Each phrase, gaze, or silence carries an emotional charge that can include or exclude, pacify or agitate, depending on the quality of intention driving it.

When speaking of Quantum Communication, an expanded perception of reality is invoked, where everything is interconnected and any movement—however small—instantly reverberates in the relationship network. In this scenario, the sender is not just someone transmitting information, but a co-creative agent of the relational field, subtly influencing the system with their energy, judgments, memories, and desires. Understanding this relational dimension of communication leads us to assume a new ethics of expression: prioritizing empathetic listening, responsibility for words, and sincere intention to restore harmony. By integrating this broader awareness, we are challenged to abandon automatic, defensive speech patterns, often inherited from family and cultural histories marked by exclusion, inverted hierarchy, or disrespect. In their place arises the need to cultivate language more connected with principles sustaining healthy systems: belonging, order, and balance. This transformation begins within—recognizing our communication mode reflects our internal state and directly influences the surrounding environment's health. Attentive listening, respectful silence, words that welcome not accuse, all become instruments of reconnection with life and the other. Thus, communicating ceases being trivial and reveals itself as a spiritual path, an exercise in active love, where each communicative gesture is a seed sown in the fertile soil of the human field, capable of germinating into understanding, reconciliation, and mutual growth.

The central premise of this approach is that every form of communication carries a vibration, an energetic quality reverberating in the systemic field and affecting all its members. The words we choose, the tone of voice we employ, the facial expression we adopt, the body posture we maintain – all are permeated by the emotion and intention residing within us at that moment. A word spoken in anger carries a different energy than the same word spoken with compassion. A thought of judgment emitted silently towards someone creates a different resonance in the field than a thought of acceptance. This vibrational dimension of communication is often perceived intuitively – we feel the emotional "charge" behind someone's words, perceive tension in the air even when nothing is said. Recognizing this reality makes us aware of the profound impact our communication has on others' well-being and the system's overall health. Communication laden with judgment, accusation, or exclusion can literally "sicken" a relationship or family environment, creating energetic and emotional barriers. Conversely, communication springing from presence, respect, and the intention to include and connect has the power to dissolve tensions, heal old wounds, and strengthen bonds of love and trust.

Given this inherent power of communication, learning to use a "systemic language" becomes essential, a way of expressing oneself aligned with principles of order, belonging, and balance governing healthy systems. This language differs radically from reactive, defensive communication patterns often learned in families and society. The first principle of systemic language is focus on responsible observation instead of accusation. Instead of pointing fingers and saying "You always criticize me!" (an accusatory generalization likely generating defensiveness), we can choose to describe observed behavior and express our own feeling: "When I hear you say X about my work, I feel criticized and hurt". This communication form maintains responsibility for one's own feeling, describes observable facts, and opens space for dialogue, rather than initiating an attack.

The second principle is inclusion instead of exclusion. Systemic language always seeks to acknowledge everyone involved's place and validate their perspectives, even amidst disagreement. It avoids generalizations ("You men are all the same", "Nobody in this family understands me"), labels ("He's selfish", "She's crazy"), or exclusion sentences ("I don't want anything to do with you anymore"). Instead, it seeks language honoring history, acknowledging bonds (even difficult ones), and aiming to integrate separated system parts. For example, instead of complaining about a previous partner, acknowledging their place and importance, especially if children are involved, is an act of inclusion benefiting the entire system.

The third principle is striving for bond restoration instead of destruction. Even in conflict or hurt situations, systemic communication's underlying intention is, whenever possible, finding a path towards reconciliation and re-establishing respectful balance.

This involves willingness to recognize one's share of responsibility, express sincere regret when pain was caused, ask for and offer forgiveness (understood as releasing resentment), and seek solutions respecting everyone involved's needs and dignity. Communication ceases being a weapon to become a bridge.

The transformative power of systemic language can be illustrated through concrete examples. Phrases weakening systems include: blaming others for one's feelings ("You make me feel terrible"), victimizing oneself ("Nobody cares about me"), making childish demands ("You have to take care of me"), disrespecting hierarchy ("I know what's best for you, Mom"), denying belonging ("He's no longer part of our family"). In contrast, phrases strengthening systems and promoting healing might include: taking responsibility ("I'm sorry I hurt you"), expressing gratitude ("I thank you for everything I received from you"), acknowledging reality ("I see your pain"), restoring hierarchy ("Please bless me in my choices, Dad/Mom", or simply, "You are the big one, I am the small one"), including the excluded ("You also belong in our hearts"). These "solution sentences," frequently used in Family Constellations, are not magic formulas, but verbal expressions reflecting an internal movement of recognition, respect, and realignment with the Orders of Love.

It is fundamental to understand, however, that effective communication goes far beyond the words we utter. Conscious silence can be one of the most powerful forms of systemic communication. In a noisy world valuing incessant talk, learning to be silent – not as passive withdrawal, but as active, receptive presence – is revolutionary. Silence can create necessary space for deep emotions to surface, insights to arise, the other to feel truly heard. Maintaining respectful silence before someone's pain or fate, without trying to fix or advise, can be an act of profound love and recognition. Silence allows the systemic field itself to "speak" and reveal its wisdom.

Complementary to conscious silence is the practice of active and empathetic listening. Listening systemically is not just registering words, but tuning into the whole person – their emotions, unexpressed needs, body language, and even systemic dynamics possibly speaking through them. It's listening with an open heart, without judgment, interruption, preparing one's defense or next argument. It's offering the other the gift of our full attention and genuine desire to understand their perspective. This type of listening has a powerful energetic effect: it validates the other's experience, strengthens the bond, and can, by itself, be profoundly healing, allowing thc pcrson to feel seen and belonging.

This new conscious listening and speaking, anchored in presence and the intention of connection, radically transforms our way of being in relation with others and the world. By cultivating communication honoring what is, without judgments or denials, we access a deeper field of human bond—a space not seeking to win arguments, but restoring relationship wholeness. In this place, each word becomes an invitation to truth, each silence a gesture of reverence, and each encounter a real possibility for healing. Thus,

Quantum Communication reveals itself not just as a relational skill, but as a path of consciousness expansion, where listening becomes an act of love and words instruments of transformation.

Chapter 14
Circles of Influence

The relational reality we are immersed in comprises multiple layers of belonging, each directly influencing how we think, feel, and act. Although the family of origin is the first field shaping our bonding patterns, it is in the present we experience, renew, or perpetuate these influences, through participation in a living, dynamic network of interpersonal connections. These contemporary relational systems are not mere contexts where life happens, but living fields interacting with us in a constant flow of energetic, emotional, and symbolic exchanges. Recognizing the complexity of these circles and their role in our self-knowledge and transformation journey enables us to move from a passive, reactive stance to more consciously assuming the place of co-creators of our bonds.

This perspective shift invites us to deeply observe environments we frequent, relationships we nurture, and roles we play in them. Each circle of coexistence—whether familial, professional, affective, or communal—represents a relational universe with its own dynamics, accumulated histories, and implicit rules influencing our behavior. How we feel upon entering these spaces, how we interact with people within them, even the type of thoughts tending to arise in our minds in these contexts are clear indicators of the energetic and emotional quality such systems offer us. This often subtle, intuitive perception is a valuable resource for distinguishing environments nurturing our vitality from those draining it. Realizing some circles operate from toxic or unbalanced patterns gives us the opportunity to reassess how we position ourselves within them and even the need to reconfigure our participation. Conversely, recognizing circles promoting belonging, mutual support, and personal growth allows us to value and strengthen these bonds, investing in them with more presence and awareness.

Understanding Circles of Influence therefore implies accepting we neither live isolated nor are affected solely by inherited ties. We are constantly shaped by networks we choose to inhabit and roles we play within them. This influence network functions as a multifaceted mirror, reflecting both our wounds and potentials, unresolved learnings and emotional maturity achievements. From this awareness, mapping systems comprising our lives and evaluating their resonance with our current values, limits, and needs becomes possible. This practice, besides therapeutic, is strategic: it allows aligning our relational energy with more authentic, healthy purposes, enabling flourishing of more balanced, true relationships. By actively assuming responsibility for our presence in these circles, we begin influencing the collective field more positively, contributing not only to our well-being but to transforming the systems we are part of.

The first step in this recognition is a mental mapping exercise: what are the main circles composing my current relational universe? Family, naturally, remains a central circle, be it origin (parents, siblings, relatives) or constituted (spouse, children). Primary dynamics learned there often continue echoing. But alongside it, other circles exert enormous influence. Work or the professional sphere constitutes a complex system, with formal and informal hierarchies, specific organizational cultures, networks of alliances, competitions, collaborations, and rules (often unwritten) about how things work. We spend much time immersed in this field, directly affecting self-esteem, financial security, sense of purpose. Friendships form another vital set of circles. We might have different friend groups, each activated in distinct contexts or representing varied identity facets. They are systems we choose (at least theoretically) offering support, mirroring, challenge, or belonging. For many, the intimate romantic relationship forms a particularly intense bi-personal system (or sometimes more complex), with its own history, communication patterns, exchange balance. And finally, we belong to broader communities and social groups – neighborhood, common interest groups (sports, arts), religious or spiritual communities, study groups, online networks – each functioning as a field with specific norms and influences.

It's fundamental to understand each of these circles operates as a distinct systemic field. Each possesses its own "atmosphere," an energetic signature felt upon entering. Think of the difference between feeling in a tense work meeting versus a relaxed gathering with close friends. Each field has implicit rules about what can be said or done, which emotions are allowed, who holds more power or influence. Each field carries collective memory of significant events occurring within it. And, crucially, each field directly affects us on emotional, mental, energetic levels. Certain work environments might generate chronic stress and inadequacy thoughts, while others stimulate creativity and collaboration. Some friendships might leave us feeling nurtured and understood, while others leave us exhausted or involved in gossip and drama. The romantic relationship can be a source of deep connection and growth or a battlefield of conflicts and resentments. Becoming aware of each circle's differentiated impact on our internal state is the first step towards more effectively managing our energy and well-being.

With this awareness, we can start applying the systemic lens developed to observe internal dynamics of each circle. What are predominant communication patterns in my work environment? And in my closest friend circle? Is there openness for honest dialogue or do unspoken things and manipulations prevail? How are conflicts generally handled in each system? Avoided, rapidly escalating to aggression, or is there constructive resolution attempt? What roles do I usually play in each circle? Always listener, leader, joker, critic, peacemaker? Are these roles flexible or rigid? Do they serve or limit me? How is the balance between giving and receiving in my friendships, work, community? Do I feel fair exchange or often perceive myself giving more than receiving, or vice-versa? And what is the predominant energetic sensation experienced when participating in each circle? Do I feel expanded, contracted, energized, drained, safe, threatened? This attentive observation allows identifying disharmonious fields in our lives – circles marked by chronic tension, lack of respect, persistent imbalance, or exclusion patterns. Recognizing these fields as problematic is the first step to deciding how to deal with them: seek transformation, establish clearer boundaries, or, in some cases, consider withdrawing.

A particularly revealing aspect of this observation across circles is perceiving how present dynamics often mirror unresolved patterns from our family of origin. It's as if we carry relational scripts learned in childhood and repeatedly enact them on new stages with different actors. How we handle authority figures at work might directly reflect our relationship with parents. Types of friends attracted might mirror dynamics with siblings. Conflicts or dependency patterns in our romantic relationship might be an almost exact repetition of what we observed in our parents' marriage. Reader, reflect: what parallels can you identify between dynamics of your current circles and your family of origin? Recognizing these mirrorings isn't cause for guilt or resignation, but a precious self-knowledge opportunity. Realizing we're repeating a family pattern at work or with friends gives us the chance to understand it better and choose to act differently in the present, breaking the repetition cycle.

This exploration of influence circles leads to an important conclusion about systemic health. Our well-being depends not only on "resolving" the past with our family of origin. It is actively influenced, day after day, by the quality of our active bonds in various circles frequented. We might have done deep healing work regarding family history, but if we remain immersed in a toxic work environment or unbalanced friendships, our systemic health remains compromised. Therefore, cultivating healthy present relationships – based on mutual respect, honest communication, exchange balance, support for individual growth – is as crucial as processing past issues. This requires discernment to choose companions and environments, courage to establish healthy boundaries, willingness to invest time and energy nurturing bonds that benefit us. Systemic health is a continuous dance between honoring roots and cultivating a flourishing relational garden in the here and now.

In summary, mapping and observing our circles of influence with a systemic lens is a fundamental self-awareness practice. It allows clearer sight of how different relational environments we inhabit affect us, identifies where unconscious patterns (often mirroring family of origin) are at play, assesses health and balance of current bonds. This awareness returns power to make informed choices about where and how we invest precious relational energy, making us more active, responsible participants in co-creating a more harmonious life aligned with deepest values, not just regarding the past, but mainly in the continuous present.

Chapter 15
Transgenerationality

We are part of an invisible network of bonds extending far beyond our individual biography. Our psychic and emotional identity forms not just from direct experiences, but is shaped by deep currents of memory and feeling connecting us to preceding generations. Transgenerationality reveals our lives are traversed by silent inheritances: unprocessed events, unrecognized pains, interrupted or wronged fates remaining vibrant in the family field, influencing us subtly or explicitly. We are not just isolated individuals trying to "be happy," but living links in an ancestral chain, carrying both resources and burdens of family history. Understanding this dimension is essential for comprehending certain life aspects seeming immune to logic or conscious effort—recurring pains, failure patterns, emotional or relational repetitions imposing themselves as enigmas. Approaching this territory with respect and openness grants access to a valuable source of self-knowledge and reconnection with our roots.

Each family possesses an emotional field operating like a miniature collective unconscious, sustaining beliefs, loyalties, pains, and silences transmitted through generations. Often, what seems a "personal problem" is actually a symbolic manifestation of something unresolved in the family system. Persistent sadness might echo ancient unlived grief. Professional blockage might root in loyalty to an ancestor who lost everything. Self-sabotage pattern might reveal unconscious repetition of a painful fate. This transmission occurs not just through words or direct coexistence; it happens also via emotional, energetic, even epigenetic pathways, composing a subtle tapestry structuring part of who we are. Becoming aware of these plots gives us the chance to name what was only symptom, welcome what was excluded, thus transforming the relationship with the past and our own history.

Facing transgenerationality means not imprisoning oneself in the past or carrying guilts not belonging to us, but recognizing marks within us from stories not starting with us—and precisely because of that, not needing to end with us. Lucidity about this dimension offers possibility to interrupt unconscious repetition cycles, free our children from these invisible inheritances, truly honor ancestors by giving new destiny to what was previously pain, silence, or exclusion. It's a path of loving differentiation, where we can internally say: "I receive what came before, with gratitude, and now choose to tread a freer path, from the life given me." When we sustain this movement with presence, respect, responsibility, space opens for life's flow to circulate again with more lightness and authenticity. Rescuing belonging, restoring interrupted orders, releasing blind loyalties return sovereignty over our own destiny, allowing us to be conscious authors of a new narrative within the lineage we are part of.

The roots of this transgenerational inheritance are diverse and frequently interconnected. On a macro level, we have collective and historical traumas. Wars, genocides, political or religious persecutions, natural disasters, deep economic crises, pandemics, colonization or slavery processes—these cataclysmic events leave indelible marks not only on social memory but also on the psychic field of families experiencing them. Constant fear, loss of loved ones, destruction of homes and livelihoods, humiliation, need for extreme survival strategies – all generate profound emotional impact which, if not adequately processed and healed, can transmit to subsequent generations. Descendants might inherit diffuse anxiety, basic distrust towards the world, difficulty thriving, or a sense of grief or anger they don't understand, silent echoes of suffering lived by ancestors in times of collective crisis.

On a more micro, but no less powerful level, we have specific family history traumas and secrets. Each family field carries marks of significant events disrupting life's natural flow or violating Orders of Love. Premature deaths, especially of children or young parents, leave pain that, if not fully lived, can "freeze" the system. Suicides, often shrouded in shame and silence, create vacuum and guilt seeking expression. Abortions, spontaneous or induced, when unrecognized and unincluded, can generate feelings of emptiness or relationship difficulties in siblings or parents. Secrets about paternity, unrevealed adoptions, committed or suffered crimes, sexual or emotional abuses, humiliating financial bankruptcies, stigmatized mental illnesses, exclusions of members for moral or social reasons – all these events create energetic "knots" in the family field. The silence, denial, shame often surrounding them act as fuel perpetuating their hidden influence, compelling descendants, unconsciously, to repeat, compensate, or expiate these unresolved events.

It's crucial to understand this transgenerational influence operates predominantly as an invisible field, transmission occurring below consciousness's radar and often in total absence of explicit narratives. We don't need intellectual knowledge that our grandfather went bankrupt or a great-aunt was excluded to be affected. Transmission happens on a subtler, energetic, emotional level. We might absorb the atmosphere of fear or sadness lingering in the family during childhood, without understanding its origin. We might learn behavior patterns (handling money, expressing affection, resolving conflicts) by unconscious imitation of parents, who in turn learned from their parents. We might feel energetically "entangled" with an ancestor's fate through invisible loyalty, feeling their emotions or repeating their difficulties as if ours. Some epigenetic research even suggests traumas can leave chemical marks on our DNA or its expression, influencing predisposition to certain physical or psychological conditions. Regardless of exact mechanism, the fact observed in systemic practice is the unresolved past remains alive in the present, influencing us through this invisible transgenerational field, whether we know it or not.

Concrete manifestations of this invisible inheritance are as varied as human life itself. One common form is fate repetition. We might find ourselves choosing partners making us suffer similarly to how our mother suffered with our father. We might face inexplicable career blockages, exactly like a grandfather who never realized his potential. We might struggle with chronic financial difficulties mirroring our lineage's poverty history. Another frequent manifestation is physical or psychological symptoms. Certain diseases might have family incidence beyond pure genetics, indicating possible systemic entanglement. Irrational fears (phobias), chronic anxiety, recurring depression, or addictions can echo unprocessed traumas or pains from previous generations. Behavioral patterns can also have transgenerational roots: tendency towards self-sabotage might link to inherited unconscious guilt; difficulty allowing oneself pleasure or success might be loyalty to ancestors who suffered greatly; explosive aggression or extreme passivity might repeat family models. Even recurring dreams with ancestral figures or strange bodily sensations can signal transgenerational influence.

How can we then begin identifying these transgenerational bonds in our own lives? The main key is paying attention to patterns seeming disproportionate or unexplained by our personal history. When an emotional reaction is much more intense than the current situation warrants, when difficulty persists despite conscious efforts to overcome it, when a physical symptom defies clear diagnoses, when we feel carrying weight or sadness not seeming ours – these strongly indicate potential connection to transgenerational dynamics. The next step is investigating, with curiosity and without judgment, our family history, even with fragmented information. What were significant events? Who had particularly difficult fates? Who was excluded, forgotten, wronged? What were major fears, beliefs, unrealized dreams in our family? Juxtaposing this information (or lack thereof, which is also significant) with unexplained patterns in our own lives, we can start perceiving subtle connections, invisible threads linking us to this inheritance.

The ultimate goal of bringing these transgenerational influences to light is not finding culprits in the past or feeling victim of immutable fate. The purpose is liberation, stemming from awareness and respect. When aware a suffering pattern or difficult feeling carried might echo the family past, this awareness itself initiates differentiation. We begin being able internally say: "This is too big for me. This belongs to you, my ancestors". The second essential step is respect. Honoring ancestors' fate means accepting it as it was, without wanting to change it, judging them, crucially, feeling blind need to repeat it out of loyalty. We can say to them, in our heart: "I see you. I honor your fate. I receive life that came through you with gratitude. And now, with your blessing, I ask permission to do differently, follow my own path". This internal movement of recognition, respect, differentiation has power to dissolve entanglements, free us from burdens not ours, reconnect us with lineage life force healthily. Honoring the past without being trapped by it opens space to live the present with more freedom, responsibility, joy.

Chapter 16
Invisible Loyalties

Invisible Loyalties act as silent forces guiding decisions, shaping behaviors, and influencing life trajectories without the individual having clear awareness of their origin. This mechanism is deeply rooted in family dynamics, sustained by a type of love expressed through the unconscious repetition of pains, failures, and difficult fates from previous generations. These bonds, though invisible, have a powerful presence, operating like silent affective contracts established in childhood, when the need for belonging to the family system overrides the instinct for self-preservation or self-realization. The child, in their archaic logic, interprets that only by suffering like their parents or ancestors can they maintain the bond with them, be accepted, and prove their love. Thus, repeating suffering paradoxically becomes a gesture of loyalty and love.

These hidden fidelities, although based on genuine feelings like love, gratitude, and the desire for connection, often perpetuate dysfunctional dynamics hindering personal flourishing. The individual feels tied to patterns they don't understand, reproducing difficulties not belonging to them or unconsciously limiting possibilities for success, health, and happiness so as not to "surpass" those who came before. The internal logic of these loyalties follows not adult rationality but operates on the symbolic plane, where suffering can mean communion with the family clan. There's an implicit belief that overcoming an ancestor's fate would be betrayal, or that healing a family pattern would require someone to continue carrying it. Thus, unknowingly, the person sacrifices their own freedom to remain "faithful" to another's suffering.

Recognizing the existence of these loyalties is the first step towards transformation. They indicate not weakness, but the strength of deep bonds that, when brought to consciousness, can be reframed. The work of liberation from invisible loyalties implies not rejecting or forgetting ancestors, but honoring their history without repeating their burdens. It is possible to maintain love and respect for those who came before without compromising one's own journey. Transforming blind love into conscious love means choosing, with maturity, to follow a path honoring the life received, but also respecting the uniqueness of one's own destiny. It's a choice of continuity with autonomy, where the past is integrated and revered, without becoming a prison. In this movement, the individual affirms their freedom to be, while also broadening the field of healing for the entire family system.

The psychological root of this dynamic lies in the archaic thinking of the inner child, often operating according to an implicit exchange logic: "If I suffer as you suffered, father/mother, then you will love me more, then I will truly be your son/daughter"; "If I don't allow myself to be happier or more successful than you, grandfather/grandmother, then I will be honoring your difficult life"; "If I carry this illness or burden for you, perhaps you can be free". These beliefs, obviously, are not consciously formulated. They operate on a deep, pre-verbal level, like a kind of soul contract made in childhood out of a desperate need for connection. Blind love cannot discern that true love requires neither sacrifice nor repetition of suffering. It confuses loyalty with imitation. Thus, out of distorted fidelity, the descendant may feel unconsciously forbidden from exceeding certain limits of happiness, health, or success not achieved by those who came before and whom they deeply love.

The manifestations of invisible loyalties in daily life are vast and often disconcerting, challenging logic and conscious willpower. One common form is carrying burdens not belonging to us. Children might take excessive financial responsibility for immature parents, feel chronic sadness actually belonging to a depressed mother, or develop paralyzing anxiety echoing fears of a war-veteran grandfather. The person feels constant weight, unexplained exhaustion, as if fighting a battle not their own. Another frequent manifestation is self-sabotage and repetition of failures. Individuals who, despite being intelligent and capable, seem always to find ways to ruin projects, lose jobs, destroy relationships, or squander money might be unconsciously loyal to a parent or ancestor who failed or believed they didn't deserve success. It's as if an inner voice says: "I cannot be more successful than you". Limiting one's own happiness is another painful consequence. People whose parents or grandparents had very hard lives may feel unconscious guilt experiencing joy, pleasure, or personal fulfillment. They might boycott promising relationships, avoid growth opportunities, or maintain chronic pessimism, as if happiness were betrayal to those who suffered. They remain "small" and unhappy to symbolically "keep company" with loved ones in their suffering. In more severe cases, invisible loyalty can lead a person to fall ill in place of another. They might develop physical or psychological symptoms similar to a sick family member, as deep identification and unconscious attempt to alleviate the other's burden by "sharing" the illness. And, in extreme situations, identification with a tragic fate can lead to following the ancestor into difficulty or even death, through risk-taking behaviors, recurrent accidents, or suicidal ideation, in desperate, unconscious attempt to reunite or atone for something for the other. It's crucial to reiterate: in all these manifestations, the person acts moved by this loyalty without awareness of the true motivation behind feelings, choices, behaviors.

How, then, can we begin identifying these invisible ties in our own lives or those close to us? Certain signs can alert us. The presence of symbiotic bonds, with extreme difficulty separating and individuating from parents or other relatives, often masks deep loyalties preventing the person from following their own path. Persistent patterns of self-sabotage or failure in important life areas, despite conscious efforts to change, strongly indicate unconscious forces, possibly loyalties, are at play. Chronic, unexplained feelings of guilt, weight, sadness, inadequacy, or unworthiness can also echo inherited burdens or loyalty to difficult fates. Paying attention to very strong internal resistance to making positive changes, as if something binds us to the current state of suffering, can reveal hidden fidelity. Asking honest reflective questions also helps: "Do I allow myself to be happier than my parents?", "Do I feel I carry a burden not mine?", "For whom do I feel pity or a need to 'save' that prevents me from caring for myself?". Observing tendency towards co-dependent relationships or assuming the universal caretaker role can also be a clue.

The good news is, however powerful, invisible loyalties can be transformed. The path involves replacing blind love, binding us to others' suffering, with conscious love, honoring the past while freeing us to live the present. The indispensable first step is awareness. Recognizing the possibility of acting under invisible loyalty breaks the spell of unconsciousness. Next comes the internal movement of honoring the ancestor and their fate with respect. This means looking at the person and their history, however difficult, and internally saying "yes" to what was, without judgment. Accepting that was *their* fate, not ours. From this place of respect, we can begin the differentiation process. We can use "release phrases" or internal affirmations expressing this new posture. For example: "Dear father/mother/grandfather/grandmother [or other ancestor], I see you and honor your fate [mention specific difficulty, if known]. It was heavy for you. I am sorry. But that belongs to you. I am just your descendant. I received life from you and thank you. With your blessing, I now choose to follow my own path. Please look kindly if I have a different fate, if I allow myself to be happy [or successful, healthy, etc.]". Repeating these phrases with intention and feeling can profoundly dissolve entanglement. It's also fundamental to reaffirm one's own place as son/daughter, grandson/granddaughter, etc., and take responsibility for one's own life, choices, consequences. Focusing on gratitude for life received, regardless of lineage difficulties, connects us with strength and reminds us the best way to honor those before is doing something good with the gift given.

In conclusion, invisible loyalties are love bonds that, operating in unconsciousness and blindness, end up generating more suffering instead of healthy connection. They keep us trapped in scripts not ours, limiting potential and perpetuating pain cycles through generations. The journey to transform blind love into conscious love is an act of courage, maturity, profound self-respect. It requires looking into family history shadows without fear, recognizing hidden dynamics clearly, having boldness to choose our own destiny, even if different or "greater" than ancestors'. Doing so, we betray them not, but honor them in highest possible way: living fully the life given us. Freeing oneself from invisible loyalties is essential step to reclaim autonomy, joy, power to co-create reality more aligned with our true essence.

Chapter 17
Illness as Message

The experience of illness, from the perspective of Systemic Psychology, reveals itself as a multifaceted and profoundly significant phenomenon, whose origin may extend beyond biology into the subtler layers of family relationships, transgenerational memories, and systemic imbalances. More than an accidental interruption in life's natural course, illness can be understood as an expressive channel through which the body attempts to communicate concealed truths, silenced pains, and unrecognized bonds. This approach does not ignore medical aspects but proposes a broadening of perspective, allowing symptoms also to be seen as reflections of a relational mismatch crying for attention. The body, in this context, ceases being just a battlefield against pathogens to become a sensitive mirror of unresolved tensions within the family system.

From this viewpoint, illness is understood as a messenger that, instead of merely causing suffering, seeks to restore order where it was broken. Physical, emotional, or mental symptoms can signal the presence of exclusions in the system, entangled bonds, or imbalances in the fundamental orders of love, such as hierarchy and belonging. Often, the body symbolically sacrifices itself in the name of blind love, unconscious fidelity to an ancestor, or an attempt to compensate for an unprocessed injustice. Thus, a symptom might carry the energy of a family secret, unlived grief, or pain suppressed for generations. What could not be said, lived, or acknowledged finds expression in the body, in a silent, insistent attempt to bring to light what needs seeing for healing to occur – not just individual, but systemic.

In this scenario, the stance towards illness needs transformation. Instead of just fighting it, the invitation is to listen to it, interpret its symbolic language, and welcome what it tries to reveal. This listening is not passive, but active and reflective, done with humility and willingness to dive into deeper layers of personal and family history. The process involves sincere, sensitive questions opening inner pathways: what part of my history or ancestors' history does this symptom seem to represent? What unexpressed emotions does it translate? What imbalance does it denounce? What movement of reconciliation or inclusion does it ask for? By welcoming these questions, space opens where illness can cease being just pain and become also a portal: an access point to consciousness, inner realignment, reconnection with vital flow. In this space of listening and understanding, suffering can paradoxically convert into healing and wisdom.

This view challenges the purely mechanistic health approach, tending to focus on biochemical or structural dysfunction of the affected organ or system. Without denying the fundamental importance of biological factors and medical care, the systemic perspective broadens the picture, suggesting body and psyche can become stages where unresolved relational and transgenerational dramas are enacted. An illness might emerge as the visible expression of deep systemic entanglement. Perhaps the symptom is "giving voice" to a family member excluded or forgotten, forcing the system somehow to "look" at that pain or injustice through the current member's suffering. Consider a child developing severe asthma in a family where an earlier baby sibling died and was never mentioned again – the child's breathing difficulty might unconsciously echo the one who "couldn't breathe" and whose pain remained suspended in the family field. Other times, illness might directly reflect a violation of the Orders of Love. A person assuming excessive responsibilities, placing themselves above parents or trying to control everyone's life (violating hierarchy), might develop heart problems or high blood pressure, as if their body were literally overloaded. Someone living in a relationship with extreme imbalance in giving and receiving, feeling constantly exploited or exhausted, might manifest chronic fatigue syndromes or digestive issues. A persistent feeling of non-belonging, linked to exclusion in family history, might manifest as autoimmune diseases, where the body seems to "attack itself". And, as seen in the previous chapter, illness can directly manifest invisible loyalty, where the descendant, out of blind love, falls ill "in place of" or "along with" an ancestor with a similar fate. In all these cases, the symptom is not the primary cause, but the visible consequence of a hidden systemic dynamic.

In this context, the body reveals itself as a messenger of incredible wisdom. It doesn't lie. While our conscious mind can create narratives, rationalizations, defenses to avoid painful truths, the body registers and expresses systemic reality directly, undeniably. Chronic muscle tensions, persistent pains, organ dysfunctions, dominating emotional patterns – all can be read as symbolic language, communication from deepest layers of personal and family history. Recurring throat problems might link to unsaid words, secrets kept in the system. Skin conditions might reflect boundary and contact issues in relationships. A feeling of weight on shoulders might indicate burdens carried for others. Illness thus becomes not just biological event, but phenomenon laden with meaning, window into hidden dynamics governing us. Learning to listen to this body language opens us to deeper understanding of ourselves and our systems.

But how can we effectively "listen" to the message a symptom might carry? The systemic approach offers a path through reflective questions, helping us shift from illness victim to curious, respectful investigator. Faced with persistent symptom, we can initiate internal dialogue (or with systemic therapist) exploring questions like: "When exactly did this symptom appear? What other significant events were happening in my family system or relationships then?". Timing often offers important clues. "What does this symptom prevent me from doing? Which life areas does it limit?". Frequently, symptom-imposed limitation points to area where perhaps we exceeded limits or followed path not truly ours. "What does this symptom force me to do? Perhaps rest more, ask for help, turn attention inward?". Illness can be radical call for life posture change. Questions more directly linked to systemic dynamics are also crucial: "If this symptom could speak, what story would it tell about my family?". "Is there any deep emotion – sadness, anger, fear, guilt – I feel associated with this symptom, even if seemingly illogical in my current life?". The key loyalty question: "To whom or what am I being loyal with this pain, illness, limitation?". And the question seeking broader meaning: "What is trying to be revealed, seen, included through this symptom?". It's not about finding immediate or easy answers, but keeping questions open, allowing insights and perceptions to arise over time, through dreams, body sensations, synchronicities. It's patient, respectful listening process.

Proposing this reading of illness as message, it's absolutely fundamental to avoid two dangerous pitfalls: oversimplification and blaming. The systemic perspective offers no ready answers or simplistic cause-effect relations like "all stomach pain means X". Each system is unique, symptom meaning only unveiled within that specific history context. Furthermore, most importantly, this approach must never be used to blame person for being ill. It's not saying individual "chose" or consciously "created" their illness. Systemic dynamics and loyalties operate on deep, unconscious levels. The intention seeking illness's systemic meaning isn't finding culprit (in oneself or others), but fostering understanding, compassion, possibility of integration. Seeking meaning should be act of love, self-knowledge, not self-judgment or self-flagellation. It's essential remember systemic perspective complements, not replaces, conventional medical and therapeutic care. By welcoming illness as messenger, we open internal space for type of healing beyond symptom resolution: healing touching existence meaning, honoring ancestral stories, recognizing previously denied bonds, allowing individual repositioning within system with more lightness and belonging. This movement doesn't guarantee immediate illness disappearance, but often brings relief, peace, new relationship with one's body and life. Listening to symptom's message is therefore gesture of courage, humility before mystery of our history, invitation to reconcile with what was, while opening space for what might become.

Chapter 18
Systemic Prosperity

Prosperity, as a concrete expression of vital flow in our lives, is directly influenced by systemic dynamics acting silently yet decisively on our paths. It results not only from individual effort or favorable external circumstances, but also from harmony with the family soul's deep movements and the orders of love governing human bonds. Prospering, in this sense, means not just accumulating goods or achieving professional success, but being attuned to a field of abundance manifesting when there is belonging, inclusion, balance, and recognition of all who came before. Persistent scarcity, recurring failures, and feelings of limitation often symptomize disconnection from this field. These difficulties point to unresolved histories in our system of origin, continuing to influence decisions, emotions, results, even unconsciously. The key to accessing a prosperous life lies in ability to honor the past, recognize excluded or forgotten ones, accept, with humility and respect, each family member's fate. When we look with love at those before—whether they failed, got rich, sacrificed, were judged—we create space for stagnant energy to circulate again. Prosperity arises when we abandon judgments, assume our place in the system, accepting life and all it offers. Systemic understanding reveals abundance isn't imposed by force or control, but invited through reconciliation with inherited stories and emotions. Thus, success ceases being ego imposition, becoming natural reflection of belonging and reconnection with origin.

Understanding prosperity this way also means revising how we relate to giving and receiving. Often, we learn to give limitlessly, as unconscious attempt to be seen or loved, while having enormous difficulty receiving, due to fear, guilt, sense of unworthiness. This imbalance compromises abundance flow, preventing life from fully reciprocating. Opening oneself to receive is act of maturity, internal reconciliation: recognizing our value, allowing enjoyment of what's just and necessary, thanking, without fear or resistance, what comes. When we give what we can with integrity and receive with gratitude, we align with the third order of love—and at this point prosperity flourishes as legitimate expression of systemic balance in our lives.

One main systemic mechanism potentially obstructing prosperity links to family exclusions. When family members with extreme financial fates – someone enriching dishonestly and morally "condemned" by family, or someone losing everything tragically seen as failure – are excluded from system memory or heart, tension field created. Descendant might unconsciously feel prospering would "betray" family (aligning with "dishonest" or surpassing "failure") or success would separate them from group. To maintain implicit belonging, they might self-sabotage chances for financial or professional success. Energy excluded with family member seems create vacuum hindering healthy abundance flow to those after. Unconscious guilt is another powerful prosperity blocker. This guilt can have diverse systemic origins. Might be inherited guilt for injustices committed by ancestors acquiring wealth, descendant feeling no right enjoy something obtained at cost of others' suffering. Might be "survivor guilt," person feeling bad having more success or easier life than parents/siblings facing great difficulties. Might be guilt for "abandoning" family's humble origins upon social/financial ascent. Whatever origin, unrecognized guilt operates as internal brake, leading person unconsciously punish themselves through financial losses, bad professional choices, chronic inability retain money or enjoy possessions.

Intimately linked to guilt is invisible loyalty to failure or scarcity. As seen before, blind love can lead us repeat difficult fates of ancestors. If grew up in family where predominant narrative was constant struggle, scarcity, financial failures, negative view wealth, might internalize loyalty to this pattern. Unconsciously, might believe to continue belonging, being loved, need remain in difficulty place. Thus, even if prosperity opportunities arise, find ways sabotage them. Might fear earning more than parents, fear family rejection if stand out financially, simply repeat mismanagement pattern or risky choices leading ancestors ruin. This loyalty to "not having" is one most common, ingrained prosperity blockages. Additionally, internal posture of disrespect or arrogance towards parents or origin can systemically interrupt life flow received from them. As prosperity is one manifestation this vital flow, disconnection from source can reflect in material, professional difficulties.

Besides these relational dynamics, we are profoundly influenced by beliefs and phrases about money and success transmitted in family, often for generations. These phrases function as mental programs running in unconscious, shaping perception, behavior towards prosperity. How many heard repeatedly sayings like: "Money is dirty", "Who has much, stole or exploited someone", "Better poor and honest than rich and dishonest", "Money doesn't bring happiness", "Our family is simple folk, never be rich", "Money causes fights, separates people"? These beliefs, absorbed in childhood as absolute truths, create internal conflict when prosperity possibility arises. Generate fear wealth, guilt earning money, distrust successful people, tendency associate prosperity with problems or loss important values. While these unconscious programs aren't identified, questioned, they continue limiting abundance potential.

Systemic view invites redefine prosperity not mere accumulation goods, but healthy, balanced vital energy flow, manifesting also materially. In this sense, prosperity intrinsically linked third Order Love: balance between giving, receiving. Abundance flows when able give world gifts, talents, work with generosity, integrity, simultaneously able receive in return recognition, fair remuneration, opportunities, resources due us, with openness, gratitude, without guilt. Many prosperity difficulties arise from imbalance this flow. Some struggle "giving" value world, due fear or insecurity. Others, perhaps more commonly, have enormous difficulty "receiving". Feel uncomfortable being paid for work, don't know accept help or gifts, minimize achievements, feel undeserving. This inability receive, often linked unconscious guilt or invisible loyalties, blocks prosperity inflow. For abundance circulate, both hands – giving, receiving – must be open.

How then can we work dissolve these systemic blockages, restore prosperity flow? Path involves, firstly, recognizing, including all family fates related money, success, without judgment. Look who won, lost, honest, not, giving each place history. Secondly, need consciously identify, question limiting beliefs inherited about money, wealth, success, choosing replace them with beliefs supporting abundance, deservingness. Thirdly, fundamental investigate, seek release unconscious guilt or feeling unworthiness preventing receiving. Might require deeper therapeutic work, perhaps constellations or other systemic approaches. Fourthly, need actively cultivate ability receive, practicing gratitude for what already have, allowing self accept what life offers good, whether compliment, help, fair pay, recognizing own value. Fifthly, essential seek balance exchanges professional, personal life, learning give sustainably, receive appropriately. Finally, work on internal reconciliation with parents, origin, cultivating respect, gratitude for life received, as this opens floodgates for all life flow, including prosperity, reach us.

Integrating these understandings, practices into daily life, prosperity ceases being distant ideal or privilege few, becoming natural consequence internal movement reconciliation, belonging. Aligning with life flow transmitted by ancestors, with humility, reverence, begin inhabit more authentic place within selves—place deservingness, balance, peace. In this fertile soil, abundance flourishes lightly, not end itself, but living expression restored internal order.

Chapter 19
Romantic Relationships

Intimate romantic relationships operate as a deep expression field for dynamics inherited from family systems, functioning not just as affective exchange space between two individuals, but as arena where emotional memories, invisible bonds of past generations resonate. Every romantic involvement implicitly brings presence of two lineages, whose histories, conflicts, exclusions unconsciously influence how partners meet, connect, coexist. From this perspective, challenges faced in romantic relationships aren't isolated events, but reflections ancestral network remaining alive, active in each interaction. It's in this system intertwining that repetitions, conflicts, blockages emerge as signs something needs seeing, recognizing, including. Thus, love life reveals itself fertile ground for manifesting hidden loyalties, symbolic reparation attempts, belonging searches transcending individual, extending to entire family system.

Engaging with someone, we not only open heart new connection, but also allow manifestation movement reconciliation or repetition old stories. Happens because unresolved emotional experiences in family origin – like abandonment, rejection, betrayal, violence, losses –

create in us kind "magnetic field" unconsciously attracting us similar dynamics. Romantic love intensity, far from just affinity or destiny matter, often relates potential that bond has activate unconscious contents, awakening old wounds, dormant patterns. Thus, initial passion might just be gateway deeper journey, where called look stories parents, grandparents, ancestors, recognizing how much they shape reactions, expectations, affective choices. In this dive lies transformation opportunity: becoming aware these influences, create internal space make freer, mature choices. Systemic love understanding invites, therefore, see each partner not as "savior" from needs, but mirror showing what still needs healing within us, our system. This view demystifies romantic ideal completeness, brings forth more realistic, profound perspective: other came not fill voids, but reveal where wounds are. With this awareness, can begin cultivate relationships sustained mutual respect, acceptance each one's life stories, commitment joint growth. For this possible, fundamental abandon impulse resolve, through partner, what belongs history with parents or ancestors, assume responsibility own trajectory. Only then relationship ceases being stage unconscious repetitions, transforms fertile space conscious love, where two whole adults meet, support, flourish together, honoring past without being imprisoned by it.

One fundamental insight systemic view relationships is our affective choices rarely as free or rational as we'd like believe. Often attracted partners who, mysteriously, allow relive or attempt "resolve" fundamental emotional dynamics family origin. Unconsciously seek what's familiar, even if familiarity involves pain or dysfunction. How learned about love, trust, intimacy, conflict, communication early childhood, observing, interacting parents, caregivers, creates internal mold, relational "map" tend follow partner searches adulthood. If grew up security, affection environment, tend seek, create similar relations. But if primary experience marked abandonment, criticism, control, instability, might repeatedly attract partners reediting same patterns, unconscious attempt, this time, get different result or finally understand, integrate original experience. Invisible loyalties parents play particularly strong role partner choice, relationship dynamics. Might seek spouse qualities admired father or mother, conversely, choose someone treating same neglect or criticism received childhood, attempt finally get missing love or approval. Woman whose father absent might feel attracted distant, unavailable men, repeating fruitless search pattern. Man whose mother excessively controlling might involve dominant partners or, opposite extreme, seek passive women trying avoid pattern, but without resolving internal issue. Furthermore, loyalty can manifest self-prohibition: if parents had unhappy marriage or one suffered greatly for love, might unconsciously feel no right be happier than them, sabotaging own promising relationships stay loyal family suffering.

Another powerful unconscious motivation is attempt heal family system through romantic relationship. Childish, omnipotent fantasy we can, through current partner, "fix" what broken family origin. E.g., person with alcoholic father might feel irresistibly attracted partners dependency problems, unconscious attempt "save" them, symbolically save father. Someone from fragmented, conflictual family might project unrealistic expectation create perfect, harmonious union onto partner, compensating past lacks. These attempts doomed frustration, place burden not belonging partner, relationship. Healing family origin wounds needs happen within own family history context, through internal work recognition, acceptance, differentiation, not through instrumentalizing current relationship. Trying use partner resolve parent/grandparent issues violates systemic orders, creates more entanglement.

These unconscious dynamics often manifest recurring dysfunctional patterns relationships. Emotional dependency, e.g., one or both partners feel can't live without other, excessive fusion nullifying individuality, often roots unresolved symbiotic bonds mother or father, deep affective need originating childhood. Betrayal repetition, perpetrator or victim, might link infidelity models seen family, family secrets extramarital affairs, abandonment traumas generating unconscious fear fully committing bond. Fear intimacy or commitment might be loyalty parents separated, ancestors tragic love fates, defense against pain repeating family suffering pattern marriage. Difficulty maintaining healthy bonds, jumping relation relation or staying clearly destructive ones, usually points multiple entanglements family history preventing person finding place as adult capable loving, being loved balanced way.

Begin unraveling these patterns, transforming romantic relationship dynamics, essential practice self-observation with systemic lens. Need ask honestly: What was my place, role family origin? How this role repeats my intimate relating way? Am I seeking partner supply needs actually inner child's towards parents? What communication or conflict resolution patterns learned home am I replicating now? How deal partner's family origin? Can respect their bonds, place own system, without trying compete or exclude them? How's giving, receiving balance our relation? Am respecting correct order, e.g., regarding previous partners or children other unions? This self-investigation, done without guilt but clarity, helps become aware systemic influences acting on us, begin differentiating from them.

Great promise systemic perspective applied romantic relationships is possibility transform them conscious spaces mutual healing, growth. When both partners willing look own family histories, recognize how influence couple dynamic, new path opens. Involves each assuming responsibility own entanglements, projections, stopping blame other for pains or frustrations. Implies learning differentiate what belongs present relation from what's family past reedition. Requires practice systemic communication, honest, respectful, seeking understand, validate other's perspective, even disagreement. Fundamentally, demands conscious respect Orders Love within partnership: ensuring dynamic balance giving, receiving; honoring arrival order regarding previous bonds; guaranteeing both belonging, respect origins families, establishing healthy boundaries protect couple space. When these elements present, relation ceases being minefield unconscious repetitions become safe container where mature love, seeing, accepting other as is, with history, everything, can flourish.

In conclusion, intimate romantic relationships perhaps most faithful, challenging mirror internal systemic dynamics. Confront us deepest patterns, hidden loyalties, oldest wounds. Yet, precisely this intensity lies immense transformative potential. Applying systemic view understand invisible forces acting affective choices, behaviors, committing cultivate relationships based consciousness, mutual responsibility, respect fundamental life orders, can break suffering cycles, co-create partnerships true sources love, growth, healing, not just ourselves, but reverberating positively systems whole.

Chapter 20
Inner Constellation

Reaching deeper understanding systems shaping lives—family ties, ancestral patterns, invisible orders sustaining or blocking love flow—inevitably recognizes such dynamics aren't limited external or relational sphere. Reflect, perpetuate also inner world, psychic images, rooted feelings, unconscious impulses acting silently, decisively. Inner Constellation emerges natural unfolding this awareness journey, proposing way access, reorganize these forces within ourselves. Approach recognizing internal field as vibrant mirror larger family system, where symbolic representations affective bonds, significant experiences, forgotten identity fragments found. This intimate space, often neglected, reveals fertile arena healing movements, reconciliation, self-strengthening.

At Inner Constellation core principle we carry, within psyche, living presence parents, siblings, partners, ancestors, various parts selves—from wounded child protective adult, inner saboteur compassionate caregiver. These internal presences don't operate isolatedly; interact, conflict, seek recognition, belonging, form invisible alliances, create complex configurations influencing choices, behaviors, emotions.

Consciously turning this field, access affective cartography allowing observe, phenomenological clarity, hidden forces acting daily life. Process, invited occupy compassionate witness posture, able see what moves behind automatic reactions, persistent fears, repetitive patterns carry, often without understanding origin. Inner Constellation practice therefore concrete opportunity cultivate sincere dialogue inner world, recognizing, honoring voices, images, sensations emerging when place self presence what still needs seeing. Not about escaping pain or forcing solutions, but allowing internal dynamics come light, find new place within us. Listening, acceptance environment, becomes possible perceive what seemed obstacle might contain legitimate call inclusion, resisting part perhaps just waited recognition, internal reconciliation significant figures can pave way new freedom being. Transformative power this practice resides precisely simplicity invites look, feel, accept—allowing, from fundamental presence gesture, internal field find, itself, new possibilities balance, belonging, peace.

Fundamental premise Inner Constellation is psychic world not empty space, but vibrant field containing internalized representations all significant people, marking events, aspects own identity. Carry within images, sensations associated parents, siblings, partners, children, ancestors, also emotions like fear, anger, joy, abstract concepts success, health, purpose. These internal representations not mere passive memories; interact each other, forming dynamic system reflecting entanglements, loyalties, resources, unrealized potentials. Like external systemic field, inner field possesses own intelligence, seeks balance, integrity. Inner Constellation method make this internal field visible consciousness, allowing observe dynamics, facilitate movements towards greater harmony.

How then engage this practice? Process begins defining clear intention. What specific issue wish explore? Persistent feeling (anxiety, sadness), repeating behavior pattern (self-sabotage, difficulty saying no), physical symptom, blockage life area (professional, affective), specific challenging relationship? Focused intention helps direct exploration energy. Next step creating conducive space, external, internal. Find quiet time, place, undisturbed, dedicate moments relax body, calm mind, center attention present moment – perhaps through conscious breaths – essential create necessary receptivity (recalling Presence importance discussed Chapter 12). Once receptive presence state, can invite imagination, body perception evoke internal representatives key elements issue. Exploring conflict partner, visualize internal image self, partner. Issue unexplained fear, represent self, fear itself (perhaps form, color, body sensation). Dealing family issue, summon internal representations parents, siblings, other relevant members. Important allow these representations arise spontaneously, without forcing, censoring. Might be sharp visual images, also abstract symbols, localized body sensations, simply inner "knowing" element presence, position. Exact representation form less important than ability connect energy or feeling carries.

With representatives present inner space (mentally visualized or felt body), next phase phenomenological observation, free judgments. Where each representative located relation others? Proximity or distance? Looking each other, ignoring, backs turned? Predominant sensation emanating each representative? Tension, sadness, anger, love, indifference? How "I", internal observer or self-representative, feel relation configuration? Specific body sensation associated any representative or overall dynamic? Phase, not try analyze or interpret, just observe, feel, allowing internal field reveal own truth, own spatial, emotional configuration. Attentive observation allows directly experience systemic principles own being. Perceive, e.g., part self (perhaps wounded "inner child") feels completely excluded, invisible internal scene, crying belonging. Notice internal representation places self inadequate hierarchy position, perhaps trying "care" parent representation, or dominated "inner critic" assumed excessive place. Feel profound imbalance interaction different parts or representations, one giving too much, other just receiving, constant conflict preventing healthy exchange. "Seeing", "feeling" these disorders internally, Orders Love understanding ceases theoretical, becomes lived experience, paving way possible reordering movements.

Fruits Inner Constellation practice multiple, profound. Frequently, clarifying insights arise pattern or feeling origins, as internal configuration reveals connections rational mind didn't perceive. Experience healing reconnections, perhaps feeling love, acceptance flow towards self-part previously rejected, finding new way internally relate parent or ancestor images, releasing old resentments or painful identifications. Very significantly, practice bring remarkable emotional, energetic relief. Recognizing, giving place what excluded, allowing internal movement towards greater order, balance, tensions dissolve, blocked emotions flow, process, sense peace, lightness, integration emerge. Fundamentally, Inner Constellation powerful exercise self-acceptance. Invitation find, within self, compassionate presence space where all history parts, emotions, internalized bonds seen, recognized, accepted without judgment. Learn say "yes" internal reality as is, first step any transformation. Simultaneously, way access inner wisdom, intuitive, deep intelligence own systemic field knowing paths healing, wholeness. Practicing attentive listening this inner field, learn trust own perceptions more, find answers, directions coming from within. This trust inner field wisdom invites cultivate more intimate, genuine presence self, where listening replaces judgment, acceptance dissolves resistances. Space, not seek fix or correct wounded parts, but offer place, name, dignity, as would any forgotten family member. Inner Constellation, therefore, not only facilitates psychic reconciliation movements, but also strengthens being's central axis, allowing walk life more wholeness, authenticity, clarity purpose. Fertile self-encounter soil true freedom blossoms: born deep acceptance what we are, what inhabits us.

Chapter 21
Daily Practice

Integrating the systemic approach into daily life requires more than mastering concepts or therapeutic techniques; it demands a continuous commitment to transforming one's gaze, listening, and presence in all spheres of daily experience. What was previously studied as theory or experienced in specific constellation sessions becomes a permanent lens, accompanying our actions, reactions, and choices, even in the simplest moments of routine. By embracing the proposal to live with systemic awareness, we begin to recognize that every human interaction, however small it may seem, holds the potential to reveal deep dynamics, hidden loyalties, and unconscious patterns repeated for generations. Daily practice, therefore, is not an additional or separate exercise from life; it is life itself lived with intention, expanded perception, and the willingness to break inherited automatisms.

This practice begins with the attention we give to the present moment, the ability to observe ourselves in action without judgment, recognizing the impulses that move us and the subtle forces influencing our behaviors. It manifests when, faced with a difficult conversation or a mundane situation, we choose to pause for an instant to feel what is alive within us, identify which part of our history is being mobilized, and decide, from that place of awareness, what our response will be. Over time, this active, internal listening becomes more natural, almost like a second emotional and relational language, allowing us to access a deeper level of understanding about ourselves and the systems we belong to. It is not necessary to wait for crises to activate this mode of presence; on the contrary, it is in small decisions, daily encounters, that the muscle of systemic autonomy is built.

In practice, living with this awareness means cultivating an internal space where all voices—those of the present and the past—can be recognized and honored, but without any single one taking absolute control of our actions. It means offering a new, more balanced and conscious place to the parts of us shaped by family dynamics, cultural patterns, or painful experiences. And it also means firmly and compassionately assuming our own adult place, the one capable of choosing freely, without denying belonging nor sacrificing authenticity. Daily practice is thus a bridge between knowledge and embodied wisdom; it is the territory where theory transforms into experience, where learning solidifies into a posture towards life. By making this practice a habit, we continue our journey of transformation with solidity, presence, and maturity.

The core of this daily practice lies in bringing systemic awareness into the flow of life. Instead of reserving the systemic perspective to analyze past problems or major crises, the invitation is to activate it during routine interactions: a conversation with a spouse over breakfast, a work meeting, dealing with children, a casual encounter with a neighbor, or even observing dynamics in a supermarket queue. It's about developing a kind of "dual vision": being present and participating in the interaction while simultaneously keeping part of the attention observing the underlying relational dynamic. Who is speaking? From what place (adult, wounded child, critical parent/mother)? What emotions are circulating in the field, spoken or unspoken? What communication patterns are repeating? This continuous observation, done without judgment, is the foundation of daily practice.

A crucial aspect of this real-time observation is learning to identify the roles being played, both by others and by ourselves. In an argument, who takes the victim role? Who acts as the rescuer? Who is the persecutor or accuser? Recognizing these roles of the so-called "drama triangle" (or other relational configurations) helps us avoid being automatically swept away by the dynamic. Similarly, it's vital to perceive communication patterns in action. Are we in an attack-defense cycle? Is there a symmetrical escalation where each responds with greater intensity? Or is there a pursuit-withdrawal pattern, where one insists and the other retreats? Perceiving the pattern as it happens gives us the chance not to feed it. Furthermore, it's fundamental to tune into the field's energy. What is the atmosphere of this interaction? Is it light, heavy, tense, collaborative? What does my body feel in this environment? This sensitivity to the field provides valuable information beyond words.

Equally important as observing external dynamics is the practice of self-awareness, learning to detect moments when we are acting from an invisible loyalty or repeating a family pattern. How can we perceive this in the heat of the moment? A frequent sign is the disproportionate intensity of the emotional reaction. If a casual critique from a coworker triggers overwhelming rage or a deep sense of inadequacy in us, it's likely the present situation is merely activating an old wound or an unresolved systemic dynamic. Another sign is compulsive impulses to act in a certain counterproductive way – the irresistible need to give unsolicited advice (perhaps repeating a parental role), the compulsion to please everyone (perhaps out of fear of exclusion), the tendency to explode in criticism (perhaps echoing a critical parent). Recognizing the familiar feeling of "here I go again," as if stuck in a repeated movie, is a clear call from consciousness to awaken from automatism.

And what to do upon realizing we are entangled in a systemic dynamic or acting out of loyalty? The answer lies in the power of internal repositioning. This is, perhaps, the heart of daily practice. It doesn't necessarily involve making a major immediate external action, but rather operating a subtle yet powerful shift in our inner posture. The first step is the conscious pause: instead of reacting automatically, create a millisecond of internal space. Breathing deeply can help anchor this pause. The second step is internally naming what's happening, without judgment: "Ah, I recognize this feeling. It's my loyalty to my mother wanting me to sacrifice myself" or "I realize I've entered the victim role here" or "This is the conflict dynamic we always had at home". This simple act of naming differentiates us from the dynamic, bringing it from the unconscious to consciousness. The third step is actively choosing the adult and systemically ordered posture: connect with the most mature part of oneself and internally reaffirm respect for the Orders of Love. This might mean telling oneself: "I am just the son/daughter, I cannot solve this for my parents," or "I respect your fate, but I choose mine," or "I hold my place and my responsibility, no more, no less," or "I seek balance between giving and receiving in this situation". This adjustment in internal posture changes our energetic vibration and our way of being present in the interaction, even if no external words are spoken.

This internal repositioning then creates space for our external actions to change as well, often in surprisingly simple ways, but with great impact on the relational field. Daily practice manifests in small conscious gestures. Instead of entering the spiral of accusation, we can choose to use systemic language, describing our perception and feeling. Instead of trying to control or fix the other, we can ask an open question inviting reflection. A sincere gesture of recognition – thanking for something received, acknowledging someone's effort, respectfully mentioning an absent family member – can dissolve tensions and strengthen bonds. Learning to establish boundaries clearly, calmly, respectfully, saying "no" when necessary, protects our energy and teaches others how we want to be treated. And, as we've seen, choosing conscious silence, refraining from participating in destructive dynamics like gossip or chronic complaining, is also a powerful systemic action. It's these small daily choices, made consciously, that gradually transform the quality of our relationships.

By engaging in this constant practice of observation and choice, we are cultivating self-responsibility. We stop seeing ourselves as mere passive products of our history or others' actions and recognize ourselves as active participants, capable of influencing the systems we are part of. Every interaction moment becomes an opportunity to practice presence, identify patterns, choose a more conscious response aligned with systemic principles. This is a fundamental shift in posture towards life: moving from a reactive, often infantilized stance to an adult, conscious, responsible posture for our contribution to the relational field.

Integrating the systemic view into daily life is, therefore, an endless path, a continuous practice of learning and adjustment. There will be days when we are more conscious and others when we find ourselves repeating old patterns. The key is not perfection, but the constant willingness to return to observation, recognition, and conscious choice. By making the systemic perspective our "constant ally," we transform the trivialities and challenges of daily life into a rich laboratory for self-knowledge, relational healing, and developing our autonomy. Every small conscious interaction is a step towards a more integrated, meaningful life aligned with the greater flow of love and life.

Chapter 22
Forgiveness and Release

Contact with the systemic entanglements shaping our experiences and relationships inevitably leads us to confront dense feelings accumulated over time: unresolved hurts, silent pains, unconscious bonds with histories not belonging to us. When we begin bringing these contents to consciousness through systemic practice, it becomes evident many burdens carried are not just memories, but energetic ties continuing to influence choices, reactions, even sense of identity. At this path point, necessary, transformative space opens for forgiveness and release—not as moral gestures, but internal acts reconciliation, liberation. Process return wholeness, where cease fighting past finally inhabit it lucidity, lightness, allowing life flow again within us more truth, vitality.

Forgiveness, viewed systemically, is neither concession nor forgetting. Conscious recognition energy still invested keeping resentment alive keeps us tied event or person generated it. More than attitude towards other, gesture favor own emotional health, freedom. About breaking pain bond, letting go need be right, receive compensation, retroactively change what already lived. This type forgiveness doesn't demand erasing history, but assuming new position before it: posture respect, acceptance, above all, healthy separation. Wound existed, pain real, but no longer needs define who we are. Letting go, lose nothing; gain internal space live more presence, clarity.

Release accompanying this forgiveness movement also extends burdens assumed unknowingly throughout life—identifications tragic fates, unconscious repetitions ancestral patterns, internalization guilts not belonging us. Often, name blind, loyal love, try carry pains not ours, living limited way compensate others' suffering. Release denies not history those before, but honors it entirety, allowing each be responsible own destiny. Silent, powerful action: internal gesture loving return, affirming everyone's belonging, placing each system element proper place. This internal repositioning returns right occupy place lightly, without unnecessary weights, affirming life active choice, not inherited burden. Forgiving, releasing, recover wholeness, open self, finally, live present fullness.

Systemic view invites redefine forgiveness. Primarily, not something do for other, but something do for self. Not about denying offense, minimizing pain, declaring what happened acceptable. Contrary, first step often involves fully recognizing wound reality, injustice suffered, hurt felt. However, next step perceive remaining attached resentment, anger, revenge desire keeps us energetically chained person or situation caused pain. Like drinking poison expecting other die. Systemic forgiveness, context, conscious decision cut that energetic chain. Choose release emotional charge binding us pain, not because other "deserves" forgiveness, but because we deserve freedom. Act reclaiming own vital energy, consumed past rumination, invest present, future life.

Particularly regarding parents, ancestors, whose actions or fates might caused suffering or limitations, systemic forgiveness assumes specific nuance: often involves ability recognize their fate as was, without pretension wanting modify it. Requires deep humility, acceptance. Can look absent father, critical mother, ancestor committed serious mistakes, recognize lives were as were, perhaps consequence own systemic entanglements, pains, limitations. Forgiveness here not mean agreeing actions, but releasing energy invested fighting reality who they were or what happened. Be able internally say: "I see your path, it was as was. That belongs you. I respect your fate, even if difficult for me. Now, I choose follow my own path". This posture respect others' fate, without identification or judgment, creates healthy separation, frees us need remain trapped accusation cycles or attempt "fix" past.

Complementary forgiveness as hurt release, have concept Release (Liberação) as conscious act disentangling selves burdens, identifications carried unduly by system. As saw chapters transgenerationality, invisible loyalties, frequently assume, unknowingly, responsibilities, guilts, emotions, even fates belonging other family members. Release active movement symbolically returning these burdens origin places. Implies, first, recognizing what not ours. Perceive guilt felt unfounded actions, echoes old system guilt.

Understand deep sadness accompanying might be grandmother's unlived grief. Comprehend repetitive failure might be loyalty father. Once other's burden recognized, release movement involves "returning" it respect. Not mean accusing or confronting externally, but making internal adjustment, intention declaration: "Dear [system member], I see this burden [guilt, pain, fate] carried for you so long, out love or loyalty. Now realize belongs you. With all respect, return it place. Keep only what mine". Crucial this return movement accompanied recognition, honor pain those before. Not about lightly discarding others' suffering, but seeing, honoring, accepting cannot carry it for them. Truly honor ancestors not repeating suffering, but receiving life came through them gratitude, doing something good with it, living own potential. Release allows take correct place system – descendant, not savior or judge those before – assume full responsibility own life, destiny.

How facilitate this internal forgiveness, release process? Although therapeutic tools like Family Constellation extremely useful, internal practices can cultivate. Initial step allow self fully feel emotions associated hurt or burden – anger, sadness, fear, guilt – without repressing, also without drowning them, just observing presence. Next, useful engage internal dialogue person or situation involved. Visualize person front, express, silently heart or perhaps writing letter needn't send, everything feel: pain caused, life impact. After honest expression, then make movement recognizing other's fate, declare intention release pain bond, return any burdens assumed. Phrases like "I release you and release myself", "Leave with you what yours, keep what mine", "Follow now my own path peace" powerful internal anchors. Visualization also help: imagine hurt or burden energy dissolving or respectfully returned origin place. Throughout process, important maintain attention body sensations, noting possible changes like chest lightness, shoulder relaxation, deeper breath, indicating energetic release occurring.

Ultimate purpose forgiveness, release, systemic perspective, restore own vital energy flow. Holding resentments, guilts, carrying others' responsibilities like building dams inner river. Energy stagnates, spent sustaining hurt or weight, cannot flow freely nourish health, creativity, present relationships, future projects. Forgiving (releasing self pain bond), releasing (returning burdens not ours), actually dissolving dams. Saying "yes" life wanting flow through us, unimpeded past shackles. Reclaiming energy live fully present, build future. Process, though often subtle, invisible eyes, marks one deepest transformation movements can experience. Letting go what not ours, welcoming love what belongs us, create internal space new presence state, where past finds rest, future received confidence. Lighter, unobstructed field, not only feel more whole, also become more available life, love, purpose pulsing beyond inherited pains. From regenerated soil finally able move forward freedom, truth.

Chapter 23
Systemic Self-Healing

Systemic Self-Healing manifests as a deep process of reconnecting with our own essence, activating internal resources often remaining dormant under layers of pain, conditioning, and unconscious loyalties. When willing look within honesty, presence, access transformation space where healing not something happens outside in, but system's natural response rediscovering order, belonging, balance. Process invites assume protagonism own trajectory, recognizing each symptom, discomfort, blockage carries valuable message something needing inclusion, reorganization, release. Self-healing therefore not pain denial or perfection quest, but conscious choice establish new relationship what feel, think, live, opening space vital energy circulate again freedom, purpose.

This form self-care anchored systemic principles respecting complexity bonds, psycho-emotional inheritances carry. Within us coexist various experience layers: individual, collective memories, repressed emotions, distorted mental images, internal characters playing learned roles, often name blind love ancestors. Systemic Self-Healing acts precisely this internal field, promoting inclusion, reorganization movement. Giving place exiled parts selves, recognizing inherited dynamics, freeing selves fates not ours, begin re-establish internal coherence translating peace, clarity, vitality. Process requiring courage, also gifting freedom: freedom be who are, whole, light, shadow, without needing fight selves anymore.

Path this internal reconciliation passes through sensitive listening practice, willingness relate what emerges without judgment. Implies developing new posture towards internal states – more welcoming, compassionate, less reactive. With support simple, yet profoundly transformative practices, like conscious breathing, body movement, therapeutic visualization, intuitive writing, become active participants reorganizing psychic, energetic field. Each presence, acceptance gesture before pain, resistance, confusion opens breach where healing can insinuate. Systemic Self-Healing offers map this return center, where become able sustain firmly, tenderly own integration, inner flourishing journey.

Foundation Systemic Self-Healing lies understanding overall well-being intrinsically linked harmony internal psychic system. This inner system complex field encompassing thoughts, beliefs, emotions, memories, body sensations, different subpersonalities (inner child, inner critic, responsible adult), crucially, internalized representations family, social bonds. When inner field disordered – marked conflicts between self-parts, exclusion painful feelings or memories, unconscious identifications others' fates, confused internal hierarchy – vital energy blocked or stagnated.

Stagnation manifest emotional malaise, mental confusion, lack purpose, frequently, physical symptoms. Systemic Self-Healing, therefore, aims restore order, inclusion, balance within internal field, allowing vital energy flow freely again, nourishing all being dimensions.

How facilitate this internal reorganization? Fortunately, not depend exclusively complex interventions. Simple, accessible integrative practices exist, when cultivated regularity, intention, promote profound changes harmonizing inner field. One most basic, powerful tools conscious breathing. Bringing attention breathing act, immediately anchor present, body, exit mental whirlwind. Deep, conscious breathing calms parasympathetic nervous system, reducing emotional reactivity, creating safe internal space observe, process difficult feelings without being hijacked. Breathing functions bridge conscious mind, deeper being layers, allowing blocked information, energies surface, gently released exhalation.

Therapeutic visualization, as explored Inner Constellation, also valuable self-healing ally. Use imagination focused way create internal dialogues conflicting self-parts, seeking understanding, integration. Visualize ancestor image whose difficult fate entangled us, expressing respect, symbolically returning burden. Connect resource, strength images present lineage, visualizing energy flowing us. Imagine reintegration rejected or wounded self-part, offering acceptance, safe place heart. Visualization, being unconscious preferred language, facilitate internal reordering movements pure logic cannot reach.

Another powerful practice therapeutic writing. Take paper, pen, allow thoughts, feelings flow freely, without censorship, extremely liberating. Write diary track internal processes, write letters (needn't send) people unresolved issues (living or dead), expressing anger, pain, forgiveness, gratitude. Dialogue writing symptoms, asking message bring. Writing helps objectify internal experiences, gain clarity entanglements, give voice what silenced, consciously formulate healing, transformation intentions.

Cannot forget body dimension. Body stage systemic dynamics often manifest, also active agent self-healing. Conscious body posture evoke, reinforce internal states. Consciously experimenting postures conveying dignity, self-respect, openness receive, humility (like slight head bow respect parents or fate) generate subtle, yet significant, changes energy, perception. Similarly, conscious body movements, even simple shaking body release tension, stretching create space, dancing freely express emotions, help dissolve energetic blockages, re-establish more harmonious flow body-mind system.

Underlying all practices, find perhaps most essential ingredient Systemic Self-Healing: radical acceptance. Cultivate internal attitude unconditional acceptance towards all self-parts, history. Natural tendency reject aspects consider undesirable selves – fear, anger, vulnerability, "shadow". Similarly, tend deny, judge, want erase painful family history chapters.

However, rejection, denial create internal fragmentation, consume enormous vital energy internal conflicts, prevent true integration. Self-healing path passes, paradoxically, through welcoming what rejected. Say "yes" fear, pain, shadow, recognizing also part us, bring important messages. Look family history, even most difficult, compassion, respect, including all members, fates. Stopping fight selves, history, starting welcome everything love, energy previously trapped conflict released. Precisely this acceptance, integration movement observe body's healing response. Including rejected parts, releasing inherited burdens, restoring greater order, balance inner field, nervous system finds new safety, regulation plateau. Chronic tensions begin dissolve. Frozen emotions finally flow, processed. Body, free weight internal conflicts, systemic entanglements, direct energy repair, health maintenance. Experience then, often, palpable relief sensation, greater mental clarity, renewed disposition, increased overall vitality. Physical, emotional health emerge natural reflection growing harmony, integration inner system.

Important remember, however, healing path rarely linear. Days great clarity, progress, followed days old patterns seem return force. Moments resistance, doubt, fatigue. Systemic Self-Healing not magic formula instant happiness, but patient, persevering journey reconnecting self, own history, bond network weaving us. Real healing possibility lies willingness keep returning practice, welcome difficulties self-compassion, trust integration process, knowing each conscious step towards order, acceptance contributes whole well-being. Ultimately, Systemic Self-Healing returns power, responsibility own well-being. Teaches us, aligned universal principles governing living systems, become conscious agents own healing. Cultivating presence, non-judgmental observation, acceptance all parts, using simple practices promote internal harmony, caring inner garden, allowing life force flow freely, health, broadest, integrated sense, flourish.

Chapter 24
Quantum Reconnection

Quantum Reconnection emerges essential consciousness expansion movement, human recognizes self integral part vast, living web transcending individual, family experiences scope. Process not limited spiritual or metaphysical practice, but translates life posture anchored perception belonging something larger, invisible eyes, yet sensibly present daily existence. Transcending ego contours, personal narratives, become able perceive reality permeated intelligence field sustaining, connecting, guiding all phenomena. Tuning this field not escape act, but return center, reunion life essential dimension, manifesting silence, presence, interconnection. Such consciousness expansion allows find internal rest place not depending external circumstances, anchored intimate recognition unity everything exists.

Opening this broader dimension, establish bridge subjectivity human experience, impersonality cosmos. Consciousness, expanding beyond self limits, becomes channel through which wisdom, guidance, healing flows emerge naturally. Expanded state requires not belief specific doctrines, but willingness silence internal voices judging, controlling, resisting, allowing feeling occupy thinking space. Conscious surrender, rigid "I", "other" contours temporarily dissolve, revealing common matrix where everything interconnected. Experience this unity state not only provides relief suffering caused separation feeling, also inspires new way living, more compassionate, cooperative, attuned existence natural rhythms.

Context, Quantum Reconnection not goal achieved, but presence quality cultivated. Invites inhabit life reverence, attentive field subtle signs, synchronicities guiding us, intuitions springing inner silence. Expanded listening state, everyday becomes temple, each instant opportunity align greater wisdom permeating everything. From connection, purpose sense reveals not task accomplished, but natural expression being harmony whole. Quantum Reconnection, therefore, not replace internal healing processes, but complements, offering expanded perspective integrating human, transcendent, personal, universal, visible, invisible, continuous dance meaning, presence, communion.

Although family system first, most influential relational matrix, belonging, meaning search not exhaust there. Multidimensional beings, nested concentric connection circles expanding far beyond immediate family or community. Belong great human family, sharing evolutionary history, collective unconscious. Belong life web this planet, interconnected all plants, animals, ecosystems. Even more fundamental level, many spiritual traditions, perennial philosophies suggest belong Unified Consciousness Field, primordial Source which all existence emanates, returns. Feeling disconnected these larger fields – humanity, nature, spirit – generate profound emptiness, isolation, meaninglessness feeling, even if done significant healing work personal, family relations. Reconnection this broader dimension often what allows find true place universe, align life purpose transcending purely individual interests.

Path this reconnection passes through conscious movement consciousness expansion beyond personal pains, dramas. Implies not denying or invalidating individual experiences or family history challenges, but learning contextualize them within much vaster perspective. Like climbing mountain top: from above, valleys, obstacles seeming insurmountable when immersed them gain new proportion, see how fit much larger landscape. Perform this inner ascent, need cultivate Presence, Silence qualities explored. Mind chatter silence, heart quietude, present moment attentive presence consciousness begin disidentify limiting ego narratives, open perceive subtler, encompassing realities. Exercise temporarily transcending personal identity touch Being vastness. Cultivating emotions like gratitude existence, admiration nature beauty, compassion all beings, reverence life mystery also helps elevate vibrational frequency, tune these larger fields.

Can actively facilitate reconnection through focused meditative practices. Although each person find own form, such practice essence usually involves following internal movements, described here invitation personal exploration: Starting point always clear intention connect Life Source, Universal Intelligence, larger consciousness field, attitude openness, trust process. Next, essential anchor consciousness present, feeling body, breath, earth contact, creating safe base. From base, initiate gradual consciousness expansion. Imagine or feel consciousness gently expanding, first filling surrounding space, extending include community, country, entire planet Earth. Feel connection humanity, all nature kingdoms, Gaia itself living being. Can go beyond, allowing consciousness merge cosmos vastness, starlight, infinite space between. Expanded state, focus turns tuning Fundamental Unity. Seek feel, more than think, interconnection everything exists. Perceive same vital energy, same primordial consciousness animating universe, also flows through us. Separation perceive daily life reveals superficial illusion, can touch underlying non-duality reality, oneness. Like recognizing self inseparable wave existence ocean. Unity space, open communion Source. Simply rest love, intelligence field, feeling sustained, nurtured. Ask silent questions, remain open receive insights, clarity, guidance, not concrete words, perhaps feeling, image, sudden "knowing". Or just rest Being, absorbing peace, fullness emanating deep connection. Return this experience gentle, gradually bringing consciousness back body, environment limits, seeking maintain connection resonance heart.

Regular practice reconnecting larger field bring precious fruits integration journey. Most immediate often profound Unity sense, direct experience famous mystical affirmation "everything interconnected".

Sensation dissolves painful isolation, loneliness feeling, replacing cosmic belonging perception, compassion all beings. Another fruit transcendence egoic concerns. Touching vaster dimension, personal problems, though still real, lose some weight, urgency. Gain perspective, resilience handle life challenges greater serenity place. Connection also promotes alignment life greater flow, universal intelligence. Feel greater clarity purpose, not specific career, unique way contribute whole good, feeling guided, supported something greater selves. Finally, practice inexhaustible source inner peace, fundamental trust life, security not depending external circumstances, springing connection existence Source itself.

Important emphasize seeking "Quantum Reconnection" not mean neglecting necessary work personal, family systems. Contrary, healing, order immediate systems create more solid base open this larger dimension without getting lost. Inversely, connection universal field provides strength, wisdom, perspective necessary handle personal, relational challenges more effectively, compassionately. Two journeys complement, enrich mutually. Integrating personal, family history awareness with universal, interconnected nature awareness, approach fuller, authentic experience who truly are: unique, individual beings, simultaneously, inseparable expressions Life totality. Reconnection fundamental pillar autonomy, integration seek this journey final block.

Chapter 25
Openness to Life

Openness to Life represents culmination internal process not only dissolved resistances, also restored existence essential fluidity daily experience. Stopping war against history formed us, abandoning need control or deny aspects selves, past, create new relation reality – freer, more receptive, more connected life natural pulse. Openness arises not logical decision or willpower effort, but natural unfolding deep reintegration work done journey. Internal space previously occupied defenses, inherited fears, unconscious repetitions begins fill fuller presence, genuine disposition live now, unpredictability, beauty. Access existence dimension where simple fact being alive already, itself, sufficient, everyday transforms fertile ground growth, learning, authentic expression.

New life posture marked subtle, yet powerful shift: exit automatic emotional reactivity, enter conscious choice state. No longer driven old patterns or invisible conditionings, begin respond life more lucidity, creating space new possibilities previously inaccessible. Openness life teaches trust event flow, even when not follow expectations. Alignment real, including both pain, pleasure, silence, movement, without fragmenting before impermanence. Trust life – not external guarantees – becomes axis sustaining actions, decisions. Trust born direct experience part something larger, life not against us, but continually inviting flourishing, even challenging situations.

Accessing internal openness state, relational field also transforms. Become more available encounter other, no longer extension needs or stage projections, but journey companions, each with history, wholeness under construction. Relations based presence, acceptance replace those molded need or obligation. Body, turn, responds relief, vitality end internal wars: more lightness, energy, health. Above all, new kind movement installs: creative impulse springing being center, desiring contribute, share, manifest. Life then ceases being just something endured or managed, becomes dance – unpredictable, challenging, profoundly sacred. Essence true openness life: live heart eyes open, ready welcome what comes, offer world what are.

What truly means open life systemic perspective? Means, above all, reach place deep acceptance own history, personal, family, exactly as was. Radically different approving, justifying, forgetting pains, difficulties. Contrary, implies looked them front, recognized impact, released burdens not belonging us, finally, able say "yes" reality what happened, without more fighting against it. Abandon idealizations how life "should been", laments what lacked. Visceral acceptance past – lights, shadows – what frees us its dominion. Stopping resist what was, energy ceases spent inglorious battle immutable, becomes available only time can truly live: now.

Openness life manifests, then, renewed capacity welcome present moment presence. Be here, now, senses awake, curious what presents, willing feel what needs felt, without excessive filters fear or inherited resentment. Openness intrinsically linked systemic inclusion principle, now applied inner world. Saw how system member exclusion generates disorder, suffering. Similarly, internal exclusion – denying personality parts (shadow, vulnerability, strength), rejecting difficult feelings (fear, anger, sadness), deliberate forgetting painful history chapters – creates blockages vital flow. Life energy seeks circulate throughout being, entire history. Saying "no" part selves or past, practice, building internal dams impeding flow. Systemic integration journey essence process learning say "yes" everything belongs, welcome all parts, include all stories. Natural consequence radical internal inclusion life flows again. Where no more significant internal exclusions, vital energy circulate freely, nourishing, healing, impelling forward. Sense can affirm, profound experiential truth, life begins where resistance ends.

Crucial understand openness life not synonymous passivity or resignation. Contrary, base from which can assume active, conscious place existence. When most energy no longer hijacked internal struggles against past or selves, becomes available creative action world. Open life means engage fully, greater wholeness, inner freedom place. Active participation manifests through essential qualities. Courage one: willingness face existence inherent challenges, risk new experiences, express authentic truth, no longer paralyzed transgenerational fears or limiting loyalties. Another quality gratitude: deep appreciation life gift received through ancestors, lessons learned (even difficulties), opportunities present offers. Gratitude opens heart receive more. Fundamentally, openness expressed through love: more mature, compassionate love selves, others, life itself, love born acceptance, connection, respect systemic orders, no longer scarcity or control need. Assume active place occupy space world dignity, contributing unique talents service something larger.

Internal posture openness, acceptance, presence reverberates concretely all life areas. Decisions become clearer, aligned inner truth. Instead choosing from fear, guilt, need please others (often family dynamic echoes), begin decide based authentic values, real present moment needs, connected intuition. Relationships also transform. Relating greater wholeness place, acceptance own history, presence, attract, cultivate healthier, authentic, intimate relations. Less space projections, unconscious repetitions, more space genuine encounter between two whole beings (or integration process). Even health physical, emotional tends benefit. Release chronic tensions generated internal resistance, systemic burdens allows nervous system rebalance, vital energy flow more freely, strengthening natural self-healing, resilience mechanisms. Body relaxes, revitalizes when inner war ceases.

Can say, therefore, Openness Life tasty harvest entire systemic healing, integration journey. State emerging naturally when made peace roots, welcomed all self-parts, released entanglements binding us, reconnected existence greater flow. Living openness not mean absence challenges or pains, part human condition. Means, yes, meet challenges more internal resources, less resistance, more trust life capacity sustain, guide us. Expression conquered autonomy, capacity respond creatively reality inner peace, strength center. Ready receive life gifts, offer own gifts world, courage, gratitude, heart daring remain open.

Chapter 26
Service and Purpose

From the moment a person achieves the profound movement of reconciliation with their roots and clearly understands their place within the family system and life, a process of internal transformation begins that inevitably overflows into the world. This transformation occurs not as a result of voluntarist effort or a desire to "improve the world," but as a natural consequence of energy previously held by entanglements, unconscious loyalties, or internal conflicts, now liberated to flow with authenticity. The internal clarity obtained by embracing one's personal history, recognizing parents and ancestors as legitimate givers of life, generates an essential stability allowing the soul to expand beyond egoic demands and seek an expression that includes the other, the collective, and expanded belonging. The impulse to serve, in this context, comes not from outside, as a moral imposition or quest for validation, but springs from within as a spontaneous response to the renewed sense of being alive and connected to totality.

This internal availability to serve reveals itself as a broadening of identity itself. The person previously focused on repairing past pains or obtaining recognition through compensatory behaviors now finds freedom to express their gifts with lightness and truth. The energy once captured by unconscious attempts to correct family histories, repeat patterns, or occupy roles not belonging to them becomes a creative force available for actions promoting balance. Thus, service is conceived not as task or obligation, but as natural unfolding of existence aligned with life as it is. And it is at this point the encounter with purpose begins: no longer as goal achieved, but coherent expression of being recognized, integrated into its system. Arises, then, real possibility live integrally, potently, offering world what true, singular, valuable itself.

With this new posture, the individual understands their contribution to the world depends not on great deeds or socially exalted roles, but on the authenticity with which they occupy their place and respond to surrounding needs. Life begins to be lived not from a search for meaning, but as continuous manifestation of meaning already found. Service and purpose, therefore, arise not as external objects conquered, but internal manifestations presence state, soul peace origin, heart available life. Fertile soil, where roots honored, conflicts pacified, true service impulse germinates: serene, powerful offering collective field, born encounter personal truth, whole needs.

The key to genuine, sustainable service lies in occupying our correct place in the system, with awareness and acceptance. Often, the impulse to "help" or "serve" can be contaminated by unconscious motivations deriving from our own entanglements. We might try to "save" others as way compensate own impotence feeling or repeat caretaker role assumed childhood guarantee belonging. Might seek service recognition, validation not received parents. Might act guilt or internalized moral obligation, invariably leading exhaustion, resentment. Service springing these distorted motivations rarely effective long term, frequently creates more disorder than harmony, as starts imbalance internal place.

In contrast, service emerging someone peace history, recognizes limits, occupies place humility, dignity – whether child, parent, partner, professional – has completely different quality. Flows naturally, like river following course. Person offers gifts, resources stable center, without exhausting self, connected own strength source. Service, born right place, nourishes both giver, receiver, truly contributes larger system balance. When in place, service becomes intrinsically authentic. No longer trying be someone not are please, compensate, belong. Freed masks, inherited roles, offer world what unique, true: specific talents, singular perspective, particular way loving, relating. Authenticity mark service coming soul. Not matter contribution grandiose world eyes or happens small, almost invisible daily gestures. What matters congruence external action, internal truth. Acting integrity place, contribution powerful impact, carries essence strength. Serve authenticity allow life express through us unique, unrepeatable way.

Connection authenticity leads rethink purpose search. Live culture often pressuring "find purpose" as if lost object or specific career discovered. Systemic, integrative view suggests different approach: purpose not so much something found "out there," but something emerging from within, gradually, as do internal healing, alignment work. One path emergence reconciliation family system. Looking history acceptance, honoring parents, ancestors (strengths, weaknesses), releasing entanglements binding us, gain clarity who are, what truly matters. Lessons learned family integration journey often reveal central life themes, gifts bring share. Another essential path inner listening practice. Purpose rarely announces through great external revelations; whispers deepest feelings, intuitions, activities bringing genuine joy, meaning, what attracts inexplicably. Requires silencing external, internal noise hear subtle soul voice. Purpose reveal not detailed career plan, but call cultivate certain qualities (compassion, creativity, courage), explore certain themes, serve certain needs resonating us. Finally, purpose also emerges when consciously respond present needs. Observing surrounding world – family, community, profession – open heart, perceive where specific gifts, capabilities make positive difference. Purpose builds intersection authentic talents, real world needs feel called respond, from place.

Profound, transformative aspect journey understanding healing own wounds, become healing channels others. Traversing own recognition patterns processes, loyalty release, forgiveness, integration, develop precious internal qualities: greater presence, genuine compassion (self, others), non-judgment capacity, boundary clarity, resilience difficulties face.

Qualities radiate naturally. Simple presence, more centered, balanced, calming, stabilizing effect people, environments around. Without direct intention "heal" anyone, become consciousness, acceptance beacons. How deal own challenges more integrated way inspire, support others journeys. Sense, greatest service offer world paradoxically care own healing, integration, makes us cleaner instruments love, consciousness flow through us benefit all.

Fundamental broaden view what constitutes service or contribution. Not all need become therapists, doctors, social workers live purpose, service life. Contribution assume innumerable forms, all equally valid, necessary. Artist creating beauty, touching people souls serving. Scientist seeking knowledge common good serving. Entrepreneur generating jobs, offering useful products or services ethically serving. Parents raising children consciousness, presence, respect systemic orders rendering invaluable service future generations. Teacher inspiring students, farmer cultivating food respect earth, employee performing work integrity, kindness – all service forms. Invitation each discover, honor unique way contribute, resonating talents, passions, exercise it love, respect own path, limits, without falling trap comparisons or external expectations.

Essence, service, purpose, systemically understood, natural overflow life found center, opened flow. Not burdens added task list, but spontaneous expression gratitude life received, desire actively participate existence great web. Occupying place consciousness, serving authenticity unique gifts, allowing purpose emerge inner listening, reconciliation roots, experience profound meaning, belonging sense. Then, not just living own life fullness, also contributing, singular way, whole healing, evolution.

Chapter 27
Field Formation

Creating, sustaining systemic therapeutic field begins deep understanding responsibility involved becoming active, conscious presence any healing space. Not simple predisposition or good intentions, but real, continuous commitment building environment favoring unveiling hidden truths human systems. Field, relational, energetic phenomenon, profoundly shaped attention quality, intention, internal posture conductor. Therefore, more than applying techniques, necessary cultivate being state capable welcome, sustain, amplify what wishes emerge, respect, ethics, clarity. Field formation begins not others, but internal, silent work, where own soul listening becomes foundation space offered other.

Assuming systemic facilitator function or even applying systemic psychology principles daily life, becomes evident field quality directly depends observer's own emotional, energetic, ethical structure. Fertile field truth flourishing not established improvised or superficial way. Cultivated discipline, self-knowledge, radical presence. Preparation involves constant internal alignment practices, body, psyche care, intention purification, genuine openness unknown. Field shapes resonance; therefore, facilitator needs be, self, tuned instrument, capable vibrate human complexity without undue distortions or interferences. Field clarity begins being clarity sustaining it. Process, indispensable recognize field not just physical or psychological space, but living reality responding truth, respect, love broadest sense. Well-formed field seeks not easy or quick solutions, but offers sufficient containment, presence authentic soul movements happen, even if imply pain, loss, limit acceptance. Willingness not know, not control, serve humility what wants emerge transforms field sacred reconciliation place. Who wishes form effective systemic fields needs, first all, become fertile soil truth seeds germinate. True work beginning.

Know systemic fields exist naturally all relations. However, proposing facilitate investigation or healing process – whether constellation session, therapeutic conversation, group dynamic, even deep self-reflection moment –, can intentionally qualify field, imbuing certain qualities making safer, potent container work. Emphasized, field quality extraordinarily sensitive internal state conductor or observer. Intentions, presence, emotional clarity, own unresolved entanglements act "tuning forks" giving field vibrational tone. Hence importance understanding essential ingredients conscious healing field formation.

Pillars sustaining systemic field conducive resolution essentially same explored discussing facilitator internal posture Chapter 12, now seen active space creation perspective. Anchored Presence fundamental: facilitator (or person self-observation) needs be profoundly present body, connected earth, breathing consciously, creating stable, calm gravity center. Solid presence acts anchor field, offering safety, stability intense emotions or difficult information emerge without destructuring process. Compassionate Neutrality equally vital. Capacity welcome everything arises field – all people, fates, emotions (including considered "negative" or "morally questionable") – without taking sides, judging, trying impose own view how things "should" be. Neutrality not cold or indifferent, permeated deep compassion human experience complexity, suffering often accompanying systemic entanglements. Radical acceptance creates space truth show self without condemnation fear. Intention permeating field also determining. Most fruitful intention not "fix" client or solve problem any cost, but serve clarity, reconciliation process specific system, respecting rhythm, limits. Intention focused greater good, maintained lightness, detachment specific results. Pure intention, free facilitator ego needs (be recognized, succeed, control), allows inherent field intelligence operate freely. Underlying all, must be Systemic Love, love beyond personal affinities, love recognizing dignity, belonging right each system member, respecting Life Orders, bowing reverence fates, even most tragic. Broad, unconditional love truly nourishes field, enables healing.

Evident, therefore, field quality directly linked facilitator being quality. Sustaining space these qualities requires continuous, deep personal work. Emotional Clarity indispensable. Who proposes facilitate systemic processes others needs good knowledge own family history, worked main entanglements, developed capacity recognize, manage own emotional reactions (resonances) during work, not project contents client field. Ethical Foundation impeccable: absolute respect confidentiality, client autonomy, rhythm; honesty own competencies, limitations; humility posture recognizing facilitator process server, not master holding all answers. Ethics containment structure guaranteeing work safety, integrity.

Beyond internal state, some practical guidelines assist field formation, sustenance. Facilitator Energetic Posture important: stay centered, grounded, conscious breath, own energetic limits. Need learn "feel" client or group field without "mixing" or getting invaded, maintaining healthy differentiation. Self-care, energy cleansing practices necessary, especially after intense work. Personal, Professional Limits also crucial: clearly define work time, scope, charge fair value balancing giving, receiving, fundamentally, know recognize own fatigue, knowledge, emotional capacity limits, referring client another professional when necessary. Trying go beyond own limits desire help harmful both. Perhaps most challenging, essential guideline Unconditional Respect Others' Fate. Systemic view confronts reality not all problems have easy or "happy" solutions eyes. Sometimes, field movement points need accept loss, live limitation, recognize tragic fate without altering. Facilitator temptation might intervene "soften" reality, offer superficial consolation, force reconciliation system not ready sustain. However, true systemic help resides courage remain present reality shows self, trusting client soul strength deal own fate, respecting limits what can or cannot changed. Humility before life mystery, individual fates mark mature systemic facilitator.

Chapter, therefore, seeks prepare reader responsible action, if feel call apply acquired knowledge more actively, whether personal, professional life, therapeutic or group contexts. Call awareness deep theoretical understanding provided course valuable base, but skill facilitate complex systemic processes others usually requires additional specific training, supervised practice, above all, unwavering commitment own personal, ethical development. Initial invitation apply principles discernment, humility own life, close relations, perhaps work environment, observing effects, learning experience. Distinction between using systemic awareness daily life, assuming facilitator role formal interventions always clear.

Systemic maturity requires, above all, deep internal silence, capable listen what not being said, but reverberates intensely field. Silence not voice absence, but expanded presence—recognition often, true service rendered system not interfere, sustain love what still process coming light. World valuing continuous doing, facilitator learns containment art, sustain not-knowing dignity, offering field sufficiently safe presence it reveal paths itself. Field formation, therefore, also trust act: trust systems greater intelligence, love restorative force when unobstructed, field own capacity conduct process when internal conditions adjusted. Refinement listening, presence, turn, only consolidates when facilitator sees self, honesty, before own humanity. No field possible without recognized vulnerability. Perfection search or absolute systemic process mastery not only illusory, also counterproductive. What favors field authenticity which facilitator positions self: know self learner, maintain constant reverence state, recognize own limitations part path. Implies, often, revisit own pain, keep soul windows open other also feel authorized do so. Field, sense, becomes mirror, container—space resonating, depth, truth we all part something larger. Ethics, presence, humility intertwining field flourishes maximum potency. When three forces harmonize, no need control or rigidly conduct; field itself becomes pedagogical, revealing hidden orders, reestablishing bonds, promoting lost belonging. Thus, facilitator withdraws discreetly, not as task finisher, but one honoring cycle movement belonging everyone. Field formation, therefore, more than technique—way being world, integrity path continuing reveal each encounter, each true listening gesture.

Chapter 28
Final Ceremony

Closing profound transformation process asks recognition, presence, conscious way cross threshold between what lived, what inaugurates. Reaching moment, evident something us already irreversibly touched, amplified, repositioned. Theoretical knowledge, reflective practice, traversed journey Systemic Psychology, germinated internal changes not just translating intellectual understanding, but new being quality. What closes now more than study; symbolic finalization integration cycle, maturation, consciousness expansion. Point subjective experience meets collective marker, internal, external, becomes passage symbol. Final stage, therefore, demands not assimilation effort new contents, but presence welcome what flourished, revere path trodden, allow new meaning level install silently within self.

Symbolic ceremony proposed closing less formality, more psychic need conclude something had weight, meaning inner life. Creating ritualistic space, even intimate, personal, allows body, soul, system whole understand transformation occurred. Integration, honor gesture. Archetypal dimension us recognizes passage rites potency, benefits immensely when lived intention, consciousness. Symbolically marking cycle end, create contour, healthy limit delimiting, organizing psyche. Conclusion gesture opens space next stage, respecting time, meaning what lived. Thus, each person create own rite – not conclude learning like closing book, but like planting, fertile soil, seed what yet come.

Allowing self anchoring, celebration moment, offer self testimony. Become someone looking history reverence, validating own steps, pains, discoveries, achievements. Attitude transforms knowledge wisdom, learning legacy. Sense, closing also silent initiation new way walking life. Systemic view, cultivated journey, now becomes part existence mode, relating, acting. What begins here life permeated greater lucidity, more conscious choices, more intimate connection human relations invisible web. New gaze, rooted, sensitive, becomes internal guide, always available reference point. Renewed presence cycle ends – not termination, but birth.

Looking back, can recognize significant stages crossing. Began establishing foundations, understanding inherently relational beings, immersed systemic fields shaping, connecting invisible ways. Learned Orders Love – belonging, hierarchy, balance – natural laws governing life, relationships flow. Dived systemic unconscious, transgenerationality depths, discovering ancestors stories, fates continue echo us. Then, moved practical applications, learning develop systemic lens diagnose hidden dynamics, knowing tools Family Constellation, Inner Constellation, exploring presence, intention, conscious communication importance.

Finally, dedicated integration, focusing daily practice, old hurt release, self-healing, reconnection larger existence dimensions, culminating openness live life fuller, present way. Each journey step invitation expand consciousness, assume more authentic, responsible place life web.

Reaching point, important celebrate inner achievements might flourished process. Perhaps perceive self greater autonomy relation repetitive patterns previously governing, freedom sense conquered letting go burdens not yours. Perhaps note development emotional maturity, expanded capacity navigate relational challenges more clarity, respect, less reactivity. Certainly, developed systemic view, new capacity perceive hidden interconnections behind apparent phenomena, both own life, others'. Vision treasure accompany henceforth. Possibly, felt call greater self-responsibility, recognizing power influence systems participate. Maybe, experienced profound reconnection moments – self, roots, nature, life greater mystery. Whatever fruits harvested, large or small, deserve recognized, celebrated personal transformation milestones.

Significant transition moments, like concluding deep learning cycle like this, honored, anchored through small personal ritual, intimate ceremony marking threshold. No "right" way do; important conscious intention recognize stage end, another beginning. Perhaps feel inspired write letter self, revisiting journey, recognizing challenges overcome, thanking learnings, expressing intentions future now opening. Or maybe prefer symbolic act: light candle representing new consciousness light cultivated, plant tree or flower new growth cycle symbol, create art object capturing transformation essence, simply find special nature place, offer gratitude silence. Another possibility dedicate time closing meditation, internally revisiting main course insights, feeling integration being, blessing path ahead. Choose form most resonating soul, allow simple gesture, laden meaning, seal moment personal passage rite.

Indeed, course conclusion not endpoint, but starting point. Marks structured learning process end, inaugurates beginning new life posture. True integration happens now, continuous, living application principles each breath, interaction, choice. About taking systemic view book world, allowing inform way being parent, child, partner, professional, friend, citizen. Continue practicing presence, non-judgmental observation, deep listening, conscious communication, respect love orders, acceptance what is. Learning journey transforms now living systemically journey.

Think moment graduation, not sense receiving diploma ending studies, but original word meaning, referring "give form," "form self". Course, been "forming" self new way being, perceiving. Graduation enables enter new cycle, cycle where act more consciousness co-creator own relational reality. Armed greater clarity forces influencing, tools navigate them, now have greater choice power patterns wish perpetuate, those wish transform. More prepared participate life dance not pawn moved invisible forces, but conscious dancer, able respond creatively rhythms, partners find path.

Crossing last threshold, perceive true learning resides not information accumulation, but silent incorporation new way being world. Systemic knowledge, lived not just understood, becomes body part, speech, gestures, silences. Each daily choice becomes fertile soil knowledge flourish, each human encounter opportunity practice listening sees, gaze includes, presence honors. No more separation theory, practice, study, life: everything becomes expression same essential movement—serve wholeness, life natural flow, humility, lucidity. New horizon, systemic view operates internal compass. Promises not definitive answers, nor quick solutions human complexities. Instead, offers compassionate, courageous lens, which possible traverse challenges more surrender, less resistance. Recognizing intelligence living systems, each disorder carries belonging or reconciliation attempt, opens space wiser interventions, less impulsive, more aligned truth wishing emerge. Facilitator self, others learns, then, trust processes time, respect fates, walk side mystery, without needing comprehend completely.

Cycle closes like circle closes: wholeness, continuity. Nothing lost—what lived remains silent wisdom form, transformed gaze, more attentive gesture. Leaving formal learning space, invitation remains remain rite state, heart willing restart, everyday, new place within self. Systemic path concludes not here; just interiorizes, beginning pulse more subtle, continuous way, living frequency accompanying each step. Journey continue unfolding choices, relations, dreams, river, finding sea, ends not—just transforms.

Epilogue

Reaching end this reading, movement not closure, but opening. Because awakening systemic gaze, no more unseeing. World reveals new light, stories—those inhabiting body, bonds, silences—begin read depth transcending personal biography. Journey offered these pages ends not last word. Contrary: continues now, you, relations, most daily gestures, most unlikely encounters. Knowledge shared here not static. Living, pulsating, moving. Like fields describes, acts subtle, powerful way. Something you touched. Perhaps deep recognition facing pain didn't know name. Perhaps lightness perceiving certain weights never belonged you. Or, maybe, glimpse new existence possibility: more rooted, lucid, whole.

Book proposed not solve enigmas, but amplify them. Real human experience depth not quick resolution, but slow listening. Willingness look what forgotten, excluded, silenced—include respect. Listening transforms. Because what seen love, reorganizes. Systemic Psychology, throughout pages, revealed wisdom field beyond therapeutic technique. Relational ethics, way being world more presence, less judgment. Invitation reconciliation not just others, but parts selves, loyalty old stories, left margin. Teaches not isolated failures, but expressions larger plot, woven visible, invisible bonds crossing generations.

What said orders love, systemic unconscious, family field, quantum entanglements not distant or metaphorical concepts. Perception tools can—should—be applied real life. Looking own system more consciousness, identify where exclusions, inversions, repetitions. More than that: perform inclusion movements, repositioning, reconnection. Small gestures, simple recognitions, words spoken truth reconfigure entirely system atmosphere. Perhaps greatest gift reading possibility new existence posture. Posture who blames not, understands. Judges not, recognizes. Carries not others' burdens, honors pain where comes. Repeats not blindness, chooses consciousness. Finally, understands loving not save other, but recognize dignity, place.

Now journey done, look back, realize read not just book. Performed inner crossing. Crossing leading automatism presence, repetition freedom, fragmentation wholeness. Crossing demands not perfection. Demands availability. Courage feel, humility learn, openness transform. Each bond yours, henceforth, more conscious. Listening reach system silences. Steps deny not past, include honorably, present fertile, future lighter. Recognize self living part ancestral web, placing self place love, truth, entire network reorganizes around. When, sometime, pains return—as inevitably will—remember: nothing just personal. Nothing isolated. Everything relationship. Precisely constatation resides greatest freedom.

www.ingramcontent.com/pod-product-compliance
Lightning Source LLC
LaVergne TN
LVHW090402210926
848480LV00002B/423